Praise for *College Su₁* and Mar.

"College Survival & Success Skills 10
navigating the college experience. Stu.
_.__ this book as they begin
their college careers will find it extremely helpful. Not only does this book
give a thorough outline of the opportunities available, it also discusses how
to quickly recover from 'mistakes' before it is too late. Furthermore,
Ragins's advice about speaking with professors and academic counselors are
words that would be most beneficial to every student...This book and her
book, *Winning Scholarships for College*, would make great gifts for the
graduating high school senior and current college students... I have used
her personally as a reference to help some of the students with whom I
work."

—Angela Grant, Ph.D., assistant professor, Northwestern University

"College Survival & Success Skills 101 contains all one needs to know to be
successful and graduate from college. The information it contains will help
students get the most out of their college years and leave the university
setting as well-rounded individuals with a skill set to make them very
marketable in today's workforce. This book is a must-read for anyone who
interacts with a high school student or college student of any age: high
school counselors and teachers; parents; college personnel; and community
members involved in the college process. *College Survival & Success Skills
101* should be required reading for all college freshmen orientation classes
and for parents of college-bound students."

—Carolyn D. Jones, Ph.D., community member involved in the college
planning process for high school and college students

"College Survival & Success Skills 101 should be given to all people before
they enter college so they can take advantage of all the resources provided by
a college, and graduate with so much more than a four-year degree...If
students apply the tips in this book, they will have experiences of a lifetime
that will springboard them to an enriched life and a successful career. This
is a great high school graduation gift."

—Leslie Kulis, parent

"*College Survival & Success Skills 101* offers advice to help you on your way to success, not only in college, but also beyond. Marianne provides an easy-to-read, well-structured plan to make the most out of every college experience."

—Jean D. Jordan, dean of admission, Emory University

"*College Survival & Success Skills 101* highlights every area a college student would need to be prepared from day one. Understanding the cost concern that faces many students and parents, the use of this book will help enlighten both on pertinent concepts to make this transition achievable and attainable."

—Nikita L. Baxter, director, Visions an Educational Talent Search Program, York Technical College

"Readers will find it easier to balance academic demands with their social lives, procure employment, and avoid excessive credit card debt and other pitfalls. The college terrain is often difficult to navigate. Ragins clearly marks the academic quicksand, financial hazards, and social landmines."

—Shlawnda Calhoun, English instructor, Stephenson High School

"I first met Marianne Ragins in 1991 when she joined 149 other high school seniors, out of an applicant pool of over 58,000 students, and was designated a Coca-Cola Scholar. She and the other 4,000 Coca-Cola Scholars I have known since 1989 live the contents of this book. In my experience, success may be a bit of luck, but mostly it is capitalizing on the information and mentoring that come from so many facets of our lives. Use *College Survival & Success Skills 101* to get the most from your college experience. The table of contents alone provides a snapshot of what one may expect to experience on this educational journey. Sensational!"

—J. Mark Davis, president, Coca-Cola Scholars Foundation, Inc.

"*College Survival & Success Skills 101* is a comprehensive road map for students entering college or someone who is enrolled and not feeling like they are getting the most from their experience. This is a must-read for my high school senior. I wish we had this book for my other two children who have finished college. For me, being a college freshman was just the next year after high school. Today's kids face so much competition that if they don't put together a detailed plan, they risk wasting their college experience. Too much has changed since I was in school, limiting my abilities to effectively coach my daughter as she enters college. As a parent, I cannot invest more than $100,000 for my child's college education unless we both read this book. *College Survival & Success Skills 101* is required reading to get the best return from a college investment."

—Randall J. Wilke, parent

"Most of our first generation college-bound students need all the support and guidance that they can get since some may be missing parental counsel or a mentor's wisdom. This book will help fill-in many of the gaps caused by a lack of college experience in the extended family. *College Survival & Success Skills 101* will also help those who are the oldest in the family, the first to go in this generation, update the material their parents may have shared about their college experiences…This book provides a very comprehensive guide to not only surviving, but also thriving during the college experience."

—Philip L. Hostetter, counselor liaison, J.P. McCaskey High School

Also by Marianne Ragins

Winning Scholarships for College

College

SURVIVAL

&

SUCCESS

Skills

101

2nd Edition

TSW Publishing
P. O. Box 176
Centreville, Virginia 20122
www.scholarshipworkshop.com
TSW Publishing is a division of The Scholarship Workshop LLC

ISBN: 978-1491080566

First Edition 2008
Second Edition 2013

Printed in the United States of America

This book is available at special quantity discounts for bulk purchases for sales promotions, premiums, fundraising, and educational use. Special versions or book excerpts can also be created to fit specific needs.

For more information, please contact info@scholarshipworkshop.com or call 703 579-4245. You can also write: TSW Publishing, P. O. Box 176, Centreville, Virginia 20122.

COLLEGE SURVIVAL

&

SUCCESS SKILLS

101

Keys to avoiding pitfalls,

staying in,

enjoying the life,

graduating,

and being successful

Marianne Ragins

To my mother, Laura Ragins; my husband, Ivan McGee; and my little ones, Aria and Cameron; your love, motivation, and presence in my life keep me going.

For Gloria Laverne Solomon
As one who truly got the most from life
and helped us to get the most from ours,
your sunny smile, loving heart and
generous ways will be remembered forever
by all of your family and friends.

COLLEGE SURVIVAL & SUCCESS SKILLS 101

Introduction	14
1. Campus Resources	**18**
The Career/Development Center	18
Writing Centers	26
Academic Advisement Center	26
The Library	28
The Student Union	29
The Student Health Center	30
Other Resources	30
Top 10 Places to Find When You Arrive On Campus	31
2. Using Campus Resources to Address Special Issues, Situations, or Problems	**33**
3. Choosing a Major	**36**
Does the Major Really Determine Your Career?	41
If You're Not Progressing And Dread Going To Class, What Should You Do?	42
4. Getting the Most From Your Classes and Your Professor	**43**
5. On Track To Graduate: Time Management and Staying On Schedule	**50**
6. Strategies for Boosting Your GPA and Developing Good Study Habits	**55**
Calculating Your GPA	56
Making the Best Grades	57
Developing Good Study Habits	60
7. Getting Internships, Cooperative Education and Other Learning Experiences Beyond the Classroom	**62**
Experiential or Occupational Learning	66
Internships	66
Cooperative Education	70

Summer Jobs/Programs 72
Research Programs 72
Directed Individual Study (DIS) 74
Internships, Co-Ops, & Summer Job
Opportunities By Industry 74

8. The International Experience 84
Going Abroad – The Basics 84
Overseas Job Opportunities 87
Study Abroad 91
Immersion Programs and Intensive
Language Study 93

9. Other College Opportunities 96
University Exchange Programs 96
Double Major 97
A Minor 98
3-2, 3-1, 2-2 Programs 98
Contests & Competitions 98
Honors Program 101
Interdisciplinary Programs 102
Early Admission Programs 103
Conferences/Forums 103

10. Life After Class 105
Scholastic Honor Societies 108
Honorary Recognition Societies, Fraternities,
and Sororities Related to Field Of Study 108
Sports and Other Activities 110
Professional Clubs/Societies/Associations 112
The Campus Ministry 114

11. Getting Along With Roommates 116

12. Romantic Relationships 119

13. Fun Within the Walls 124
Special Interest Clubs 125
The Greek Life 125
College Parties and Pastimes 126

14. Working Around the Campus 129
Work Study & On Campus Jobs 130
Community Service and Volunteering 131
Professional Trade Experience &
Campus Organizations 132

15. Networking and Professional Development 136
Receptions 137
College Recruitment Conferences/Job Fairs 138
Career Fairs 139
Associations 140
Interviews 140
Information Sessions 141
Faculty and Staff 142
Graduate and Professional School Days 142
Networking Tools 143
Developing Interpersonal Skills 151

16. The Student Entrepreneur 156
Advertising & Promotion 157
Advice 158
Understanding Start-Up Costs and Other Issues 158

17. The College Investor 163
Mutual Funds 165
Saving Bonds 167
Certificates of Deposit 168

18. Building a Blue-Chip Stock Portfolio On a College
Student's Budget 169
Buying Through Discount Brokers 171
Companies Allowing Direct Stock Purchases
Without a Broker 172
Investment Clubs 173

19. Handling Credit Cards – Keys to Graduating With
Little Or No Debt 174
Common Credit Card Mistakes 175
Your Credit Report 182

20. Student Loans and Your Future   **183**
    Before You Borrow   183
    Alternative Ways of Paying Off Education Loans   184
    Why Credit Cards Are a Bad Idea for
    Funding An Education   185

21. Getting More Financial Aid to Finish College   **186**

22. I Am So Lonely Being Away From Home.
    What Can I Do?   **197**

23. Top 10 College Pitfalls and Essential Tips
    for College Survival   **201**

24. Social Media–Can It Help or Hurt Your College Life? **207**

25. Top 10 Reasons You Should Get an Internship   **212**

26. College Prep for High School Students   **214**
    What I Wish I Knew Before I Entered College   214
    Campus Advice from College Students and Recent Grads   219
    Keys to Preparing for College in High School   221

27. Final Thoughts   **224**

Appendix - Other Resources from Marianne Ragins   **226**
    Books and Publications   226
    Workshops & Boot Camps   227
    Webinars & Online Classes   227
    eBooks   228

About the Author   **229**

Index   **230**

Special Thanks

Patti Ross, Carolyn Norton, J. Mark Davis and the Coca-Cola Scholars Foundation; Bing Spitler, former manager of College and University Relations, Armstrong World Industries; Florida Agricultural and Mechanical University, and the many instructors I referenced in this book, Professor Ronald Jarrett; Dr. Ivy Mitchell; Dr. Evelyn Trujillo; Dr. Angela Grant; Jany Kay Allen; David Buckholtz; Rondre Jackson; Otis J. Ragins Jr.; Professor Tammy Hiller, Bucknell University; Professor John Miller, Bucknell University; Scott Price; Cadeltra Adams; AJ Robinson; Ryan Upshaw; Julia Rose Judge; Charity Avery; Tavia Evans Gilchrist; Spencer Blevins; Daniel Lyons; Amehlia Mehtar; Janel Janiczek; Jeannette Bennett; Jordan Scarboro; Dianna He; Hayley Ford; Roberto Lopez Jr.; Hodari Pilli Tourre Brown; Richard Rusczyk; Ashley Chang; Erin Husbands; Amy Crook; Fraya Cohen; Deneige Kay Miles; Stephen Schorn; Ivan McGee; Marcus Braswell; Nikki West; Stephanie Gargiulo, Carolyn Norton and Janice Hyllengren.

Introduction

Most students graduate from high school with visions of going to college but not with visions of how a college education can help them. Many don't know what to expect from college, or what to expect from themselves. Some students decide to attend college at the urgings of their parents; others to get away from their parents; some because of their friends; and a few for the sheer joy of higher learning. Whatever the reason, not everyone has the option of going to college. College can provide you with tremendous learning opportunities to further your personal and career development, and most other aspects of your life. However, it requires your effort and an awareness of those opportunities for you to really get the most out of it and to survive college beyond freshman year.

The total cost of a college education ranges from roughly $20,000 to well over $100,000 for four years. Wouldn't you consider it to be a waste of thousands of dollars–not to mention your time–if all you did was go to college for four or more years, and then graduate feeling no more enriched than when you arrived? Most students about to graduate and step beyond the walls of their college campus reflect on their accrued accomplishments. Some have feelings of frustration due to realizing that they have squandered four years and lost opportunities ripe with challenge and adventure. Others, who met numerous challenges and reaped the benefits of several opportunities such as an internship, study abroad, or directed individual study, feel supreme fulfillment. Attending college can open doors into worlds otherwise unknown, as those who graduate feeling satisfied *and* enriched very well know.

I have heard many college graduates exclaim, "I haven't used a thing I learned in college. The educational system is archaic. Most of my classes were boring and useless." Who wants to waste thousands of dollars and countless hours earning a degree that's useless? I am sure *you* wouldn't want to. This book will help you get the most out of your college education, aid you in recognizing unique opportunities you may only be able to experience as a college student or on a college campus, and urge you to utilize many of the resources available on your campus. It is also designed to help you avoid typical college pitfalls and give you strategies for choosing a major, getting the best grade point average (GPA), overcoming loneliness, enjoying college life, graduating with a great job offer or graduate school placement, *and* so much more. When you graduate and look back on your college years, I want you to feel enriched, enhanced, and most of all that the experience was worthwhile. You will need first to understand a college degree is not the total summation of your college experience.

Did you know that you can get college credit for volunteering in a soup kitchen or studying in London? Were you aware that you can visit a doctor, receive medical treatment, see a play, or listen to an award-winning playwright, author, or musician, discuss his or her techniques in one day and in one place—your college campus? Did you know you can get investment advice or tips on starting your own business, also while on campus? For years I dreamed of learning how to play the piano, but had neither the opportunity nor time to do it. In my last two semesters of college, I realized this dream and many more. If all you do in college is satisfy the requirements for your degree, you'll miss out on a lot of opportunities and challenges.

If you don't know how you can make your college experience all you want it to be, you will after reading this book. I have written each chapter with three goals in mind: helping you get the most from your college education, helping you avoid typical college pitfalls, and helping you succeed in your college endeavors. I have included my experiences, those of many of my friends, and those of students all over the country to illustrate how our lives have been enriched by college. My job as author of this book is to make you aware of the many resources available at college. *Your job* is to take advantage of those opportunities and use the resources available to you to make your college experience, and the rest of your life afterwards, a success.

You could graduate with multiple job offers in your pocket; numerous skills and activities on your résumé; as the owner of your own business; as the possessor of an investment portfolio; as a student with many graduate or professional schools clamoring to admit you; as a world traveler; in minimal debt . . . and much more.

Without your effort, college could very well be a waste of time and money. But with your effort, a world of opportunity awaits you. Explore it! Challenge it! Embrace it! But most of all, enjoy it!

Throughout your college career you will be constantly shaping your future into whatever you envision it to be. Your vision can encompass many areas. When you think of your immediate future, you may see graduating, getting the job of your dreams, graduate school, or fulfilling your own personal fantasies. Whatever your mind conjures up for you, chances are that somewhere on your college campus or during your college career, there is an opportunity just waiting to open its doors and help you achieve your dreams. But first, you must know where and how to look. You must find it, work for it, and then use it to your advantage to have the future you envision for yourself. If you succeed, you will have learned the true value and essence of a college education. Education has many facets and involves learning within and beyond the classroom: it encompasses the campus and its resources, your professors and their advice, your friends and their opinions, and so much more. Your overall learning experiences and your total involvement in college life differentiate the attainment of a college degree from the attainment of a complete college education.

Learning is so much more than the information in the pages of a textbook. A real college education involves tapping into every resource on your campus, as well as neighboring campuses, and campuses all over the world open to you as a student. You must explore the wealth to be found in every building on your campus, in every faculty and staff member, in every contact, in every office, and every club. If you do, you will be well on your way to shaping your future into the vision of your dreams and getting the most out of your college education.

If obtaining a complete college education is one of your goals, many opportunities await you. Explore many of them in this book, and then explore them in reality. I promise you will be thoroughly enriched by your experiences, and you will be well on your way to surviving college, but also being successful in college and out. I know I was!

1

Campus Resources

On a college or university campus there are a multitude of offices and services to assist with many of your needs and concerns. Indeed, if you know which office to consult, you may never have to go beyond your own campus. There are offices such as the career/development center to help you make career choices; launch a job search; or find a job, co-op, or internship. There are resource centers in which you can expand your leadership abilities, your writing skills, or your knowledge of mental health, for instance. If you need mental or physical treatment, you can find that too on your campus. Consult your college or university catalog or web site for information on specific offices and the services they offer.

The Career/Development Center

The career/development center is an office or building with information and individuals dedicated to providing resources to assist you in finding summer and postgraduate jobs, internships, cooperative education programs, study abroad courses, and much more. The Career Center or its equivalent should be one of the most important resources you consult when determining your career path and how you will find the job of your dreams. You should become familiar with both the reference materials in the office and the individuals who make things run smoothly. Most offices will have computers, brochures, and binders from corporate recruiters, applications, job data banks, interview signup sheets, lists of corporate receptions, interview dates, and a wealth of helpful information available to you as a current student, alumnus, or a student from a neighboring campus. Also many campuses have career centers allowing you to connect with them on various social media platforms such as Facebook, Twitter, LinkedIn and YouTube. Make sure you get connected to be alerted about opportunities at your school. These opportunities could include study abroad, internships, research opportunities and more.

At the career center you should find trained individuals skilled at helping you to determine a major, a career, and your job search criteria. They may also conduct workshops on writing résumés, successful job interviewing, taking job placement tests, completing applications, developing effective communication and networking skills, and many other topics. The career center may also offer individual counseling, career assessment tests, and videos of mock interviews. In addition to services provided face to face at the center you may also be able to attend or listen to webinars, podcasts, and other online types of online broadcasts with or without prospective employers to help you get prepared for a bright future. Most centers have or should have as their goals the following:

- To develop and enhance the marketability of the students who visit the offices;
- To provide relevant and current information to students about employment opportunities;
- To expose students to corporate professionals willing and able to provide students with employment opportunities.

Registering

At most career centers you will be required to register. To do so, you may need to complete a form listing your name, current address and telephone number, major, expected graduation date, times available to interview, and the types of jobs in which you are interested (internship, co-op, permanent placement). Most registrations are usually done online and will include you uploading your résumé to their system.

Once you have done this, update your résumé frequently and visit the office often as well. Visiting helps those in the office associate your face with your name for opportunities that may not get posted but for which student names are provided by career center personnel.

On the following pages you will see several variations of my résumé including the one I created during my freshman year, primarily for internships, and the one I used as an upperclassman.

- *Résumé Example 1* - Résumé used to obtain an internship and permanent job placement in the area of marketing and sales.

- *Résumé Example 2* - Résumé used to apply for a job at a major public accounting firm. The recruiter was specifically interested in my coursework in accounting. By the way, this résumé attests to the advantages of hanging around the career center. I had been in the career center for a while on this day after an earlier interview. The recruiter from this accounting firm saw me and started a conversation. After a couple of minutes, he asked if I would like to interview for a job in Los Angeles with his firm. I said yes. He conducted the interview and I sent him this résumé. **Note** – The objective is different in this résumé.

- *Résumé Example 3* - This is my first résumé, I used it mainly for my first internship.

Your résumé should be one page. You should also make sure that your résumé is clear and well organized. In addition, if there's a possibility your résumé will be scanned, you should use a scan-friendly format. To find examples of additional résumés (including formats that are scan-friendly) and types other than the chronological examples shown on the following pages, visit the following web sites:

- Monster.com Resume Center - http://resume.monster.com (or visit http://www.monster.com, see résumé center)
- CareerBuilder.com (http://www.careerbuilder.com, see advice and resources)

Résumé Example 1

Marianne N. Ragins

| UNIVERSITY ADDRESS | FAMU Box 00000 | Tallahassee, Florida 32307 | Telephone: (850) 555-1212 |
| PERMANENT ADDRESS | P. O. Box 0000 | Macon, Georgia 31208 | Telephone: (478) 555-1212 |

OBJECTIVE
To obtain a challenging marketing/sales position with a major corporate entity in need of an individual with extensive literary, analytical, and organizational skills.

EDUCATION
Florida Agricultural and Mechanical University—School of Business and Industry   **Bachelor of Science—Business Administration**
Graduation Date: April 1995   **Grade Point Average:**   3.8-4.0   *The National Dean's List 1991 - 1994*

SEMINARS/WORKSHOPS ATTENDED
Selling Skills; Relationship Strategies; Career Workshop; Presentation Skills; Goal Setting; Writing Skills; Diversity Awareness

HONORS/ACHIEVEMENTS
Winner of over $400,000 in scholarship awards; Cover story—*Parade* magazine, also featured in *Essence, Newsweek, Money, Jet, Readers Digest, People, Black Enterprise,* and *YSB* magazines; appeared on *Good Morning America* (ABC), *The Home Show* (ABC), *Teen Summit* (BET); January 11, 1992 declared *Marianne "Angel" Ragins Day* in Wilmington, Delaware; Coca-Cola Scholar; Life-Gets-Better Scholar; Armstrong Scholar; Wendy's Scholar; Outstanding Service Award, 1991; Letter of Commendation from Clarence Thomas, Supreme Court Justice, 1991; Letter of Commendation from Thomas B. Murphy, Speaker of the House, Georgia General Assembly, 1991; Coordinator, *Benjamin D. Hendricks Undergraduate Honors Conference,* 1993 & 1994; Panel speaker, *The 21st Century - Education Beyond the Classroom,* 1993; Mock Trial Team, Florida Collegiate Honors Conference, 1992; International speaker at the Crystal Palace, Nassau, the Bahamas 1993.

ORGANIZATIONS
Presidential Scholars Association; University Honors Council; Volunteer Coordinator for Special Olympics 1991; Volunteer speaker for local schools; Red Cross Volunteer; Director of Organization & Planning, Hometown News, 1994; National Collegiate Honors Council; Southern Regional Honors Collegiate Council; Florida Collegiate Honors Council; Invited to join the National Association of Educators; Vice-President, Junior Business Writing, Inc.

PUBLICATIONS
Author and publisher of *Winning Scholarships for College: The Inside Story;* Author of *Winning Scholarships for College: An Insider's Guide* published by Henry Holt & Co; Author of *Hourglass,* poetry and audio tape published by the National Library of Poetry.

WORK EXPERIENCE
06/94 to 08/94   **Armstrong World Industries—*Internship Assignment in Philadelphia, Pennsylvania***
Marketing Representative I
- Focused on presenting acoustical solutions to customers in the educational and health care markets of Philadelphia, Pennsylvania. Also made field sales calls for the same markets in the areas of Washington D. C., Baltimore, northern Virginia, New York City, and northern New Jersey.
- Received the **Quality Recognition Award** for independently developing a follow-up sales call form to aid distributors and future interns with their marketing efforts.

06/93 to 08/93   **EDS Belgium N.V.—*Overseas Internship Assignment in Brussels, Belgium***
Technical Assistant
- Interacted in a diverse business and personal environment composed of Belgian, Dutch, German, Irish, African, Italian, English, Spanish, and Portuguese individuals as well as many other nationalities.
- Assisted with numerous translations of Dutch, Flemish, and French into correct English grammar.
- Created financial documents and presentations for the sales, finance and government divisions.

06/92 to 08/92   **Electronic Data Systems (EDS)—*Internship Assignment in Raleigh, North Carolina***
Proposal Manager
- Entailed managing and editing material from proposal and technical writers, coordinating staff meetings and project deadlines, as well as overseeing all aspects of production concerning EDS's proposal for TIPSS.

COMPUTER PROFICIENCY
WordPerfect, Ventura Publisher, Lotus 1-2-3, Microsoft Word, Microsoft Excel, Microsoft PowerPoint, ABC Flowcharter, MacDraw, Photostyler, Freelance Graphics

References Available Upon Request

Résumé Example 2

Marianne N. Ragins

UNIVERSITY ADDRESS	FAMU Box 00000	Tallahassee, Florida 32307	Telephone: (850) 555-1212
PERMANENT ADDRESS	P. O. Box 0000	Macon, Georgia 31208	Telephone: (478) 555-1212

OBJECTIVE

To obtain a challenging finance position with a major corporate entity in need of an individual with extensive literary, analytical, and organizational skills.

EDUCATION

Florida Agricultural and Mechanical University----School of Business and Industry   **Bachelor of Science----Business Administration**

Expected Graduation:	April 1995	Grade Point Average:	3.8/4.0	*The National Dean's List 1991 - 1994*
		G.P.A./Accounting:	3.6/4.0	

RELEVANT COURSEWORK

Financial Accounting, Managerial Accounting, Intermediate Accounting I, Intermediate Accounting II, Auditing I

HONORS/ACHIEVEMENTS

Winner of over $400,000 in scholarship awards; Cover story----*Parade* magazine; also featured in *Essence, Newsweek, Money, Jet, Readers Digest, People, Black Enterprise,* and *YSB* magazines; appeared on *Good Morning America (ABC), The Home Show (ABC), Teen Summit (BET)*; January 11, 1992 declared *Marianne "Angel" Ragins* Day in Wilmington, Delaware; Coca-Cola Scholar; Life-Gets-Better Scholar; Armstrong Scholar; Wendy's Scholar; Outstanding Service Award, 1991; Letter of Commendation from Clarence Thomas, Supreme Court Justice, 1991; Letter of Commendation from Thomas B. Murphy, Speaker of the House, Georgia General Assembly, 1991; Coordinator, *Benjamin D. Hendricks Undergraduate Honors Conference,* 1993 & 1994; Panel speaker, *The 21st Century - Education Beyond the Classroom,* 1993; Mock Trial Team, Florida Collegiate Honors Conference, 1992; International speaker at the Crystal Palace, Nassau, the Bahamas 1993.

ORGANIZATIONS

Presidential Scholars Association; University Honors Council; Volunteer Coordinator for Special Olympics 1991; Volunteer speaker for local schools; Red Cross Volunteer; Director of Organization & Planning, Hometown News, 1994; National Collegiate Honors Council; Southern Regional Honors Collegiate Council; Florida Collegiate Honors Council; Invited to join the National Association of Educators; Vice-President, Junior Business Writing, Inc.

PUBLICATIONS

Author and publisher of *Winning Scholarships for College, The Inside Story*; Author of *Winning Scholarships for College: An Insider's Guide* published by Henry Holt & Co; Author of *Hourglass,* poetry and audio tape published by the National Library of Poetry.

WORK EXPERIENCE

06/94 to 08/94	**Armstrong World Industries----***Internship Assignment in Philadelphia, Pennsylvania*

Marketing Representative I
- Focused on presenting acoustical solutions to customers in the educational and health care markets of Philadelphia, Pennsylvania. Also made field sales calls for the same markets in the areas of Washington D. C., Baltimore, northern Virginia, New York City, and northern New Jersey.
- Received the **Quality Recognition Award** for independently developing a follow-up sales call form to aid distributors and future interns with their marketing efforts.

06/93 to 08/93	**EDS Belgium N.V.----***Overseas Internship Assignment in Brussels, Belgium*

Technical Assistant
- Interacted in a diverse business and personal environment composed of Belgian, Dutch, German, Irish, African, Italian, English, Spanish, and Portuguese individuals as well as many other nationalities.
- Assisted with numerous translations of Dutch, Flemish, and French into correct English grammar.
- Created financial documents and presentations for the sales, finance and government divisions.

06/92 to 08/92	**Electronic Data Systems (EDS)----***Internship Assignment in Raleigh, North Carolina*

Proposal Manager
- Entailed managing and editing material from proposal and technical writers, coordinating staff meetings and project deadlines, as well as overseeing all aspects of production concerning EDS's proposal for TIPSS.

COMPUTER PROFICIENCY

WordPerfect, Ventura Publisher, Lotus 1-2-3, Microsoft Word, Microsoft Excel, Microsoft PowerPoint, ABC Flowcharter, MacDraw, Photostyler, Freelance Graphics

References Available Upon Request

Résumé Example 3

In addition to your e-mail address you may want to include your LinkedIn
address on your résumé.

Marianne N. Ragins

Permanent Address	**University Address**
P. O. Box 0000	FAMU Box 00000
Macon, Georgia 31208	Tallahassee, FL 32307
Telephone: (478) 555-1212	(850) 555-1212

Professional Objective: Corporate lawyer for a major business entity that will utilize both my degrees in business administration and in law

Education: Presently matriculating as a sophomore at Florida Agricultural & Mechanical University's School of Business & Industry

Relevant Coursework: Honors English I and II
Principles of Accounting
Managerial Accounting
Introduction to Business Systems
Business Writing

Work Experience: **07/89 to 05/91**
Wendy's International – Macon, Georgia
Description of job duties:
- Cashier
- Elevated to gold star status in January 1991

06/92 to 08/92
Electronic Data Systems – Raleigh, North Carolina
Description of job duties:
- Proposal manager for the Tallahassee Integrated Public Safety System (TIPSS)
  - Desktop publishing, word processing and production for the following proposals:
    - North East Ohio Information Network (NEOMIN)
    - City of Garland (Request for Information)
    - The City of Savannah
    - The City of Broken Arrow
    - Indianapolis Sewer System

Honors/Organizations: Deans List—Fall quarter 91/Spring quarter 92
Phi Eta Sigma National Honor Society
University Honors Council
Presidential Scholars Association
Volunteer Coordinator for Special Olympics
Volunteer speaker for local area junior and senior high schools
Red Cross volunteer
January 11, 1992 declared Marianne "Angel" Ragins day in Wilmington, Delaware

References Available Upon Request

Making Your Face Known

Because the career center will be one of the most important resources on campus for finding a job, you should make sure the individuals who work there know you. Even if your campus is very large and the center may see hundreds of students a day, you would be surprised to learn how many students do not take the time to get acquainted with the center's staff. Most students wait until the end of their senior year to even think about visiting the center. However, if you make it a point to stop by every week, not only to gather job information from the numerous pamphlets, magazines, and brochures in the office, but to say hello, you will make a lasting impression that could earn you an interview slot with a major corporation at the last minute or a personal introduction to a recruiter while you're in the office visiting. Sometimes visiting recruiters take a group of highly qualified students to dinner. One of the ways you can become one of those students is to make sure the people at the career center know who you are, since they usually recommend the students the recruiters invite to dinner.

When to Become Acquainted with the Career Center

Although other centers may be set up differently, the career center at Florida Agricultural and Mechanical University helped students to find internships, summer programs, co-ops, and part-time employment, and assisted alumni in finding jobs. The career center on your campus may do more or less. If they do more, great! If they do less, they may be able to point you elsewhere for assistance. If they can't do that, this book is designed to help you find information on your own.

Become acquainted with the career center as early as your freshman year. Don't wait until you are about to graduate and need a job. As Whitney Young, civil rights activist and former director of the National Urban League, once said, "It is better to be prepared for an opportunity and not have one, than to have an opportunity and not be prepared." Becoming acquainted with your own or another school's career center is part of your preparation for a permanent job placement opportunity or a slot in graduate school.

Not only can the career center assist you in finding a job, they can also assist you in choosing a major appropriate to your interests and goals. Many career centers do this by interviewing you or having you complete a questionnaire. The questions asked are designed to target your primary interests and goals. Based on your answers, several majors are suggested for you to pursue. You and the career center professional then narrow it down to one. For some colleges and universities, help with choosing a major may be done through a (virtual or face-to-face) advisor or entirely online.

Many universities such as Texas A & M University maintain an online career center (http://careercenter.tamu.edu) where current and former students can access job listings from numerous companies all over the country. The online career center also provides access to job placement information, assistance in making career choices, updates about career fairs in the area, help in launching a job search, résumé-writing tips, and other career-related support. If your university does not provide similar services as Texas A & M University or you want an additional resource to help you, review chapter 15, "Networking and Professional Development."

To post your résumé online *and* get other career related information, you can use services such as the following: http://www.careerbuilder.com and http://www.monster.com. To view information about internships, visit http://www.youtern; http://www.internmatch.com; http://www.collegerecruiter.com; http://www.internships.com; and http://www.internjobs.com. If you're interested in job listings for the federal government, visit http://www.usajobs.gov.

There are many free services for researching jobs and posting your résumé online. Be wary of any requesting a fee. You can probably do an adequate job of getting your résumé out without spending any money. In fact many such services on the Internet are sponsored by the employers who use the database to find potential employees, and are free to the students who use them. Before using any database that requires payment, be sure to thoroughly research it. If you are paying your hard earned money, you want to know that the company can actually deliver what they promise. Ask your friends, relatives, and other students on campus who have used the service what they thought about it. Most importantly, go to your career center and ask if they have heard of the service and whether it is legitimate. You can also do online searches for reviews of the service.

Writing Centers

Writing skills are essential in the postgraduate world. Students who have mastered the art of writing create a distinct edge for themselves over the students who have not. In virtually all careers, communication is one of the leading factors for success and learning to write well is one of the most effective methods of communication you can acquire at college. Most universities and colleges maintain writing centers to help students improve their skills.

Skilled writing consultants are on hand to help those who visit the center with revising, mastering English as a second language, identifying consistent errors, and answering general questions. Many centers conduct regular workshops on basic grammar and punctuation, preparing thesis statements, research and documentation, and critical writing techniques. Some institutions may also offer an online writing center for students, as does George Mason University in Fairfax, Virginia (http://writingcenter.gmu.edu).

Academic Advisement Center

You should consult with your academic advisor about registration procedures, which courses to take, prerequisites for a particular course, your major, your future career, your graduation plans, and any other area where you want or need advice and assistance. If there is one, you can also consult your school's academic advisement center. This office has professionals who aid students with issues and questions surrounding the choice of a major.

Getting the Most From Your Advisor, the Advisement Center, and the Advisement Process

Use the following guidelines for getting the most from your advisor, the advisement center, and the advisement process.

- Be proactive. Don't wait for your advisor to contact you about registration, your major, your career, or any other decisions you must make during the course of your college career. You must make appointments with him or her. If you can't do it face to face, set up a virtual meeting or communicate via e-mail or texting if necessary.

- Use your advisor as one of your main contacts regarding such subjects as campus services, extracurricular activities, required courses, internships, and experiential learning.

- Before visiting your advisor, organize your thoughts and ideas. Write a tentative agenda for the time you plan to spend with him or her, listing all your questions. This way, you will be making the most productive use of everyone's time.

- Assess yourself and your abilities. Have at least a tentative idea of your goals, the direction in which you want your campus life to go, your learning ability, your major interests, and your priorities.

- Become familiar with your college catalog and the schedules of classes. You can usually review these on your university web site if they are not available paper based.

- Prepare a checklist of classes that will satisfy credit requirements needed each semester or quarter. You should be able to obtain degree audits or curriculum check sheets from your advisor or the university web site for your department. Begin checking off classes you have taken and those you still need to take and get an idea of when you would like to take the remaining courses. Your advisor will be able to help you make your selections, but remember that he or she is there to assist you–the final decision must be yours.

- Plan - As one of my professors was fond of saying, "Remember the Six P's: Prior planning prevents piss-poor performance." This is excellent advice for mastering your college experience and getting the most from it.

The Library

One of the most important resources you will find on your college campus is the library. The library is a provider of all types of information in many forms—volumes, microfilms, government documents, maps, and periodicals. They also house multimedia items such as CD-ROMs, e-books, articles, and online databases.

You can use the information you find for research, entertainment, classes, a business venture, or personal enhancement. For example, as a college investor you can research prospective companies in which to invest at the library. You can read daily periodicals such as the *Wall Street Journal* (http://www.wsj.com) and *Investor's Business Daily* (http://www.investors.com), or monthly publications such as *Fortune* (http://money.cnn.com/magazines /fortune), *Business Week* (http://www.businessweek.com), and *Forbes* (http://www.forbes.com). You can also find *Moody's* (http://www. moodys.com) and the *Value Line Investment Survey* (http://www. valueline.com). For the majority of your classes in college, you will probably have projects to complete. The library is one of the best resources for information and if you can find the perfect nook, it is also a great place for quiet study.

You may find a variety of libraries on campus tailored to certain areas of study. For example, there may be one library for business students, and a separate library for law students.

Libraries on many campuses are also very computer-friendly. Most university libraries can be accessed through your personal computer, tablet or even smart phone. Libraries also have computerized and Internet based catalogs, allowing easy access to information. The majority may also have computers with popular software programs such as Microsoft Word, Microsoft PowerPoint, and Microsoft Excel in the library's media center. In most cases, the computers will also have wireless Internet access.

If your library doesn't have information on a particular subject, it may have access to the holdings of other universities in the area. The online catalog will usually list other school's holdings. For example, colleges such as The George Washington University, American University, and Georgetown University belong to the Washington Research Library Consortium (WRLC - http://www. wrlc.org). This consortium allows students at any of these institutions and others within the consortium to borrow freely from other schools within the consortium.

The Student Union

The student union is the most comprehensive building you will find on your university's campus. This collection of buildings, offices, services, and individuals comprises the life-force of the campus. It is the community center and the focal point for virtually all student services and activities. Students can visit the student union to discuss university policies and issues with the student government president, stroll over to the cafe for a quick bite to eat, attend a meeting on women's rights, saunter into the game room for a quick bout on a popular video game, hang out in a social lounge, pick up the latest brochures on popular issues, join the Chess club, get a little money out of the bank, get a copy of the latest bestseller in the bookstore, or visit the Career Center and talk with a recruiter. How's that for a bastion of student activity!

Student unions usually contain the following (and much more):

- Cafeteria or deli
- Lounge area
- Study area
- Game room
- Student activities office

- Student government office
- Post office
- Information desk or area
- Student organization offices
- Bank or ATM
- Computer center
- Meeting rooms
- Ballrooms
- Career center

The Student Health Center

This center usually provides primary health care services. University students can often be examined at no charge for many of their health concerns. However, there is usually a fee for most tests and procedures performed. Some universities also offer health and dental plans for students not covered by their parent's medical plan or by another outside plan. If needed, the health center can also prescribe medicine or provide referrals. Some health centers allow online access to request appointments, renew prescriptions and view lab results.

Other Resources

- University information services–Access to information about the college, student resources, and events on campus.
- Health education center–May sponsor general health fairs; center may also have brochures on general health and your well-being.
- Center for new students–Helps freshman and transfer students make a smooth transition into the schools environment and quickly acclimates them to the campus.
- Center for service learning–A center for service learning promotes volunteer service among students as a learning tool. The center may also have a learning-by-doing (LBD)

curriculum that offers academic credit to students in exchange for community service or related activities. At some institutions, students are allowed to take advantage of an alternative semester or quarter break during which they can become immersed in a community project for one or two weeks. The time is used to confront and respond to social issues the students may have been focused on only in the sterile classroom environment. Issues may include AIDS awareness, Native American culture, social justice and public policy formation, environmental issues, senior services, youth education, or homelessness. Schools such as Bates College in Lewiston, Maine (www.bates.edu/service-learning.xml or http://www.bates.edu/harward) and Michigan State University in East Lansing, Michigan (www.servicelearning.msu.edu) have successful service learning programs. Refer to the chapter 7, "Getting Internships, Cooperative Education and Other Learning Experiences Beyond the Classroom," for more information about volunteer opportunities.

Top 10 Places to Find When You Arrive on Campus

1. Office or designated location to obtain your student identification card
2. Housing office or housing assignment
3. University bookstore or an online resource for purchasing textbooks
4. Registrar's office (if you need it, make sure to ask for an advisor's help with your class schedule)
5. University cafeteria and on-campus eating options particularly those with late-night access
6. Financial aid office and student accounts
7. Safe and popular places to relax and have fun along with options for Internet access (preferably high-speed or wireless)
8. Banking options, especially ATMs

9. Ways to get around the campus and the city
10. Store for purchasing toiletries, sundries, and anything else you need at the last minute

2

Using Campus Resources to Address Special Issues, Situations, or Problems

Are you a first generation student? Do you need special assistance for a learning or physical disability? Are you in need of information or counseling specifically targeted to minorities, women, or specific cultures? Do you need help resolving issues with a class, appealing a grade, or a handling a stalker? If you answered yes to any of these questions, your university campus probably has a resource you can use.

Many may have more than the service centers referenced in this chapter. The following summaries include information about other campus resources you may find helpful in resolving issues, handling special situations, and obtaining more information in a plethora of different areas.

- **University ombudsman**–For most universities, the purpose of the ombudsman is to give every voice on campus an opportunity to be heard by an impartial party (i.e. the ombudsman) without fear of retaliation or loss of privacy. An ombudsman can help students with course and instructor issues; disputes with university staff; coaching and advice for conflicts; as well as grade appeals, accusations of academic misconduct, and course repeats.

- **Counseling and student development center**–Offers personal and group counseling on a variety of subjects.

- **Drug education center**–Conducts training programs and provides individual counseling; center may also have educational material such as brochures, pamphlets, and handbooks on drugs, alcohol, and substance abuse. Information may also be available online.

- **Campus network center**–Maintains a peer educator program and offers community resource referrals; may also maintain a list of campus self-help group meetings, such as Alcoholics Anonymous.

- **Self-development center**–Conducts workshops and provides self-instruction materials such as videos, CD's, eBooks, and audio tapes for self-directed students. The center gives students the opportunity to develop new skills, assess themselves, or independently supplement class learning. Available programs may include stress management, anxiety control, study skills, time management, developing and handling relationships, test taking skills, and computer skills.

- **Multicultural and resource center**–Provides information and consultation to students and groups to promote multi-cultural understanding.

- **Child development center**–Offers child care services to students, faculty, and staff; may also offer parenting workshops and learning-based programs for the children who attend.

- **Disability support services**–Helps to integrate disabled students into campus life and academics, including assisting in the preparation of special tests, rooms, and Braille menus, or providing sign language interpreters.

- **Women's studies and resource center**–Holds workshops, lectures, and other events focusing on women's issues.

- **Academic support services**–Helps students in areas such as developing good study skills and habits, preparing for exams, and managing time wisely; may also offer academic workshop and learning skills specialists to assist students.

- **Student support services**–Offers support services to first-generation, low-income, or disabled college students; may offer workshops and other resources to help students enhance academic skills, increase retention and graduation rates, and assist with entrance into graduate and professional school programs.

- **Student leadership center**–provides opportunities for students to develop and enhance their leadership skills. May offer workshops on a variety of issues and skills such as public speaking, managing others, and planning effective meetings. Excellent resource for training aids, advice, books, and media on developing leadership skills. Center may also organize conferences on topics such as women's leadership, minority leadership, student leadership, and student services to honor individuals and provide a forum for discussions and insightful presentations on issues surrounding each area.

3

Choosing a Major

Are you worried about choosing a major? Don't let the prospect of selecting a major scare you. Although many students start college with the decision about a major already determined, there are just as many who are still undecided after a few weeks, months, or even years after hitting the college campus. In fact, there are quite a few students who change their major, not once, but several times.

If you're one of those who's still trying to settle on a major, the following tips will help you on the path to making your final decision.

Tip #1 - Consult your academic advisor. Discuss your thoughts and ideas for the future as they relate to the majors in which you are interested. However, before consulting the Academic Advisement Center or your advisor for help with your major, ask yourself a few questions. The major you choose could shape the rest of your life, or as many people discover, it could play a minimal role–if any. To get the most out of your college education, choose a major that in some way will positively affect your post-collegiate life.

Even though learning in any form is invariably life enhancing, it should have an impact on your eventual career. This is why you must put some serious thought into your college major. If you are already in college, you may even have to reassess the college or university you are currently attending if it does not offer a degree relevant to what you are interested in doing for the rest of your life.

Mark Donnelly certainly understands this situation. Even though Mark received a full-ride scholarship to attend The Cooper Union for the Advancement of Science and Art in New York, he soon realized that his heart was not in engineering. Instead, he wanted to major in business, an option that wasn't available at Cooper Union at the time he attended. Although transferring was difficult and is a task that Mark wishes students were better prepared to handle, Mark continued his college career at Stony Brook University and became a successful business owner in Ronkonkoma, New York, a small city in Long Island.

In preparing for a meeting with your advisor or the advisement center, you need to consider several factors. For example:

- *What do you want your salary to be when you graduate from college?* Majors lead to specific occupations, and those occupations can command different salaries. If salary is a primary concern to you, it should also be a primary consideration when determining your major. For example, if you major in education, your post graduate salary might not be the same as it would if you majored in computer science. Of course personal growth, satisfaction, the thirst for knowledge, personal self-worth, challenge, fulfillment, self-respect, love, and trust can't be measured by your salary. But if you believe money and the amount of it you have are determinants of your happiness, major in an area that will command a high salary for you. You can use the *Occupational Outlook Handbook*, usually found in local libraries, to get more information about various occupations and related salaries. You can also find this handbook online at http://www.bls.gov/ooh. Or you can visit http://www.salary.com as another resource.

- *In what area will you major?* Do you want a highly technical or specific major such as engineering or accounting, or a general liberal arts degree such as math or political science? General majors can be applied to many different occupations. For example, one Florida Agricultural and Mechanical University student obtained her undergraduate degree in mathematics and began her career as a business analyst at a prominent software development company in the

Washington, DC metropolitan area. As a math major, she could have pursued jobs in areas such as sales, marketing, systems management, accounting, and business management. However she explains, "What I do has absolutely nothing to do with math or anything I studied in my major. My current employer, like many other corporations, hires people who they think have the ability to do the job. They didn't really care what your major was. They even had a guy testing computer systems who majored in government! Companies will train you in what you need to know." I majored in business administration and I interviewed for and obtained job offers from a wide range of industries and occupations, including marketing, manufacturing, pharmaceutical sales, systems management, teaching, accounting, and consulting.

- *What do you enjoy doing?* This may seem like a silly question, but it's one of the most important. If you don't like your major, you probably will not do well in it. Even if you do well enough to graduate with a degree in this area, you probably won't like a job in the same field. You will probably be miserable. For example, suppose you major in accounting but you hate it. You get a job with a major public accounting firm and you hate that too. You don't get promotions because your attitude stinks. You hate the fact that you haven't moved up in ten years. Because you haven't moved up in ten years, your salary reflects it. Are you getting the picture?

- *How much time do you want to devote to your job?* When I was in high school, my fondest dream was to become an obstetrician. I loved children and I wanted to be a part of bringing them into the world. Then one of my teachers pointed out to me that babies arrive at all hours, especially odd hours like in the middle of the night, on Christmas Day, at Thanksgiving dinner, or during a dinner party. She said that unless I was willing to devote a large part of my life to my career, I probably would not enjoy my job very much. She was right. I wouldn't have—not only because of my time, but also because the sight of blood really frightens me.

If you need additional help deciding on your major, you can also consult individuals at your career development center. Speak with professors and other faculty and staff to obtain additional outlooks on the subject.

Tip #2 - Review the time it will take to earn a degree in the major that you choose. Perhaps your college funding does not extend that far. Or maybe your patience with pursuing higher education does not last that long. Four years may not be enough. If the amount of time you spend in college is important to you then you should consider time as a factor in thinking about your major.

Tip #3 - Speak to someone in the career field you are considering. Ask if you can job shadow for a day or a few days.

Tip #4 - Do some research about the major and the associated career fields. Look at books such as the *Occupational Outlook Handbook* (http://www.bls.gov/ooh); contact associations affiliated with your major and/or future career; and visit web sites such as http://www. salary.com.

Tip #5 - Volunteer at a location that offers you the opportunity to review your job prospects.

Tip #6 - Try to get an internship or co-op position in the field you plan to enter. With a co-op position you may alternate attending school with extended periods of work for a company or agency that needs students in your area of study. This period could extend from several months to a year. The company or agency you work for generally pays your tuition bill or provides a salary designed to cover your tuition bill in exchange for your services. In this arrangement your school may also give you academic credit based on the work experience you are accumulating in your field while working with the company or agency.

Tip #7 - Think about a minor as well as your major. Your minor could be your career back-up plan.

Tip #8 - Conduct your own degree audits. You should always know where you are on the path to graduation. Look at the courses required to obtain your degree. Keep them on your wall or in an easily and constantly viewed location such as the home screen of your tablet or smart phone. If you are well into your second year and the courses needed for completion haven't been taken either because you are still trying to determine a major; or because you don't want to take courses in your major; or you need to retake courses in your major because you did not do well; you should probably reconsider your choice of major.

Tip #9 - Don't let choosing a major traumatize you. Understand that you can change later, if necessary. Most students change their major at least once in college. Even though I don't suggest doing it too often or much later than your second year, it is perfectly acceptable to do so rather than getting a degree in an area only to end up pursuing a second degree or graduate degree in another field because the first was in an area you shouldn't have pursued anyway.

Tip #10 – Get involved! One of the activities in which you get involved may help you decide on a major or a future career. It certainly did for Ryan Upshaw, a graduate student at the University of Mississippi. As an undergraduate, Ryan participated in the Associated Student Body, Student Programming Board, Ole Miss Ambassadors, Mortar Board, Omicron Delta Kappa, and Lambda Sigma. He also studied abroad in London and participated in two spring break service trips with Habitat for Humanity. He says, "All of these experiences led me to pursue a Master's degree in Higher Education. I got involved because I enjoy working with people and trying to make a difference in the lives of others no matter where I am."

STUDENT HIGHLIGHT

Getting involved in activities beyond the classroom also helped Ashley Chang decide on a major and a future career path. Ashley, an undergraduate at the University of Southern California (USC), always had an interest in broadcast journalism, though her fascination with this career field intensified after two significant experiences. During her first semester as a college student, Ashley saw a flier for an open house featuring Annenberg TV News (ATVN), USC's award winning nightly student-run newscast.

After attending the open house, Ashley auditioned for an anchor position and became a weather anchor! Ashley comments, "I learned how to make my own graphics, work the chroma key, and become comfortable speaking live on-air! I also learned a lot about how a newscast works and how much work is required for a thirty-minute show!"

Then, Ashley earned an internship at *Good Morning America* (GMA) on ABC television. Ashley gushes about her internship, "Aside from working backstage at the Golden Globe Awards, attending the "Morning After the Oscars" *Good Morning America* show, and meeting several celebrities (including the cast of a major television show, Meryl Streep, Eddie Murphy, and more), this internship gave me great hands on experience in the broadcast world. I learned how to send in story pitches and research story ideas. And as I shadowed producers and reporters, I soaked in all the information I could! My experience at GMA was definitely interesting and exciting! It proved to me that internships are always great ways to learn more about the industry you are interested in! My experiences…even motivated me to add on a double major in Broadcast Journalism!"

Does the Major Really Determine Your Career?

For many people, the answer is no. There are theater majors who become sales representatives. There are math majors who become software analysts. There are accounting majors who go into the field of music. And there are political science majors who become college women's basketball coaches, such as Rondre Jackson, mentioned in chapter 14, "Working Around the Campus."

With that in mind, don't let choosing a major paralyze you. Choose an area that can enrich and enhance your knowledge. And explore all of the opportunities open to you on a college campus. Volunteer! Research! Invest! Travel! Study Abroad! Become an Entrepreneur! Along the way, you'll probably stumble upon a career that you can love for the next twenty to thirty years of your life.

If You're Not Progressing and Dread Going to Class, What Should You Do?

Once you begin to take courses in your major or volunteer or intern in a job that could lead to your future career, ask yourself the following questions: How do these courses or this job make me feel? Can I love the career that this major or this internship might lead to? If you feel great about what you're doing and you love your major and future career prospects, you're on the right path with your future career choice or major. If you dread going to classes associated with your major and the thought of actually waking up to a job that is associated with a particular field, then you should consider changing your major immediately.

4

Getting the Most from Your Classes and Your Professor

Students can easily forget that time spent in class not only brings you closer to completing your major and ultimately earning a degree, it can also help you gain more knowledge than that found in the pages of a textbook. For example, as a business administration major, I took several courses that I found absolutely boring. However, since they were required courses I never realized how much valuable information I was picking up along the way. Unfortunately, this realization didn't occur until the end of my sophomore year, but when it did, I began to make an effort to soak up information like a sponge.

You may be wondering where I am heading with this, especially since many of you probably believe a large part of the college curriculum for the first two years is core courses that can be an advanced repeat of high school. That's true. First year college courses like principles of accounting and physics, similar to those I took in high school, didn't interest me in the least until I realized they were actually helping me.

When I completed my first internship and tax time came around, I knew how to prepare my own taxes without the aid of either my parents or a tax professional. This may not sound like a big deal, but by this time I had already self-published my first book, so not only did I have income from my last internship to account for, I also had income from book sales to record. It became more than a little complicated. But with the aid of my accounting teachers, some of whom had once been practicing accountants, I sailed through them easily. Uncle Sam got his and I got back a little chunk of my own.

A college accounting course can be useful in preparing your first tax return, creating a balance sheet or income statement for a new business venture, or in calculating your net worth. If you ever need a loan for a business or other financial information, these skills are important, particularly if you can't afford a professional. And yes, there are software programs such as Turbotax and smart phone apps such as Mint (http://www.mint.com) to help you with calculating taxes and net worth but it's wonderful when you understand the method behind the calculations.

Attentive listening in an investments class could lead you to the road of sound financial management, helping you to amass a small nest egg by the time you graduate and a fortune by the time you retire. Managing your finances and investing your income are two keys to financial success. Why not take advantage of a course dedicated to it and a professor skilled in it to plan your financial future? Students at Baylor University's Hankamer School of Business certainly can. Through a course offered at the university, select students along with two professors actively manage the Philip M. Dorr Alumni and Friends Endowed Investment Fund, currently valued at $5.3 million.

If you're interested, legal environment of business and commercial law are two classes that could help you with legal matters. In both classes, you will learn the intricacies of small claims court. Classes such as these can also teach you how to write a living will or a contract, create a trust, plan your estate, or aid one of your relatives. Even if you don't learn all the details of how to write and create legal documents yourself, you will become familiar with their execution and know what to look for in the legal documents of others for your protection. Law-related classes can also help with purchasing real estate and insurance. Even if you're not really interested in law, classes such as these are helpful in real life situations. Although you may engage a professional to assist you with legal matters, such as trust funds, real estate purchases, or a will, it helps to be familiar with what they do. And, these classes and others such as the *Developing Apps for iPhone and iPad* at Stanford University in California or the course at Georgetown University in Washington, DC on Jay-Z (Shawn Carter), a prominent rapper, can be highly interesting.

Some quick tips for surviving and getting the most out of *all* your classes:

- Sit in the front or middle of the classroom. This will improve your grades for two reasons. You'll pay more attention if the professor is constantly staring you in the face or standing in front of you to make his point. From the professor's prospective, he will probably notice you more and appreciate the fact that you are listening. This could earn you more consideration when the class participation and attitude factor are figured into your borderline grade of B but an *nth* way from an A, or a D but an *nth* away from a C. Get the picture? The professor may also be willing to devote more of his office hours to help you understand a difficult concept.

- Visit your professors' offices often, when class first starts and when finals are approaching. Most students who are lackadaisical about class, sit in the back and chat, or don't go and then show up the week before finals to beg the professor for lenience in her grading policy or for extra help in understanding something it took her weeks to explain, may receive less than full concern. Monik West, currently a graduate student at George Mason University certainly agrees. She has contacted her professor many times throughout her most difficult course and states, "I strongly believe visiting the professor in her office, sometimes even on weekends has greatly contributed to my current A to B average in her course. Make use of your professor's office hours. It really makes a difference."

- Get to class on time. Show interest in the lecture. Follow the discussion. This is not only to be respectful; it also keeps you in your professors' favor, or at least out of his disfavor. Participate! Participate! Participate! And do not use your cell phone or send text messages during class.

- Ask questions. You'll never learn if you don't ask questions about concepts you don't understand. Even if you think your question is stupid, the real stupidity is if you don't ask it and then whatever you didn't understand and didn't ask about appears on a test and you are unable to answer the question.

- Lend your own experience to the class discussion. Tell the class and professor about your internship at a manufacturing plant and how the term "bottleneck" applies to both the classroom discussion and the problem you had at the plant. It will help you to remember important points if you can relate them to your experiences. It also helps your professor place your name with your face if you contribute to discussions.

- Take notes and date them. It helps you when preparing for midterms, finals, or quizzes. It is also a good idea to review your notes immediately after class or within a short time frame after the class while information is still fresh in your mind.

College is an exercise in mind control and discipline. Even though a class may seem exceedingly boring and without real life application, it's not so. College is life. College is aerobics and Zumba in mind. You will use your mind every day for the rest of your life. You might as well whip it into shape while you're in college.

STUDENT HIGHLIGHT

David Buckholtz, an alumnus of Emory University, really enjoyed his reading and writing journal course. Instead of participating in classroom discussions about people and places or discussing literary works, David and his classmates were encouraged to explore their personal histories and origins and record their observations in a journal. The class revolved around external learning factors rather than internal classroom factors such as textbooks or the professor.

David explains: "As opposed to a traditional English course, we didn't just read books about places. For the course, I traveled the Georgia barrier islands extensively as well as other parts of Southern Georgia such as the Okefenokee Swamp. My final project for the class was to travel back to Warner Robins, Georgia with my grandmother and write down my history and connection with Georgia in a journal. Warner Robins is where my mother grew up and where my grandmother spent thirty years of her life. I researched many places around Georgia to get a historical balance to my families' experience."

David feels that his experience with this class has been unforgettable, particularly in his personal development.

UNIVERSITY HIGHLIGHT

Management 101 at Bucknell University

Firsthand experience in management is the name of the game for students at Bucknell University in Lewisburg, Pennsylvania. Management 101, initiated in 1978 by Professor John Miller as an experiential general education course, committed to a balanced focus on liberal education and on preparation for professional careers in businesses and other organizations. The course is designed to provide a comprehensive overview to students who have no prior formal management education.

Management 101 companies are real management experiences, with actual customers and clients. The companies set their own business and service missions, design their own organization structures, staff themselves, and prepare a comprehensive business plan they present to the course's Board of Directors, which is made up of professors and student teaching assistants. The course begins with the Board issuing loans to the student companies, ranging from $3,000 to $5,000. The actual loan amount depends on the nature of the business plan.

During each semester, approximately four companies operate simultaneously. The companies are usually run by twenty-five to thirty-two students and average an after-tax profit of about $1,000 each. Each company is required to complete both a service project and a business project. Past student companies' business endeavors include a nightclub, a novelty playing cards venture, glassware companies, and many T-shirt and other clothing businesses. One of the most imaginative companies was Campus Sounds, a company formed to produce and distribute a compact disc of local campus bands.

The objective of the companies' service projects is to make as big a difference in the world as their creativity, sensitivity, and resources will permit. Over the years, Management 101 companies have provided a wide variety of services for groups and individuals in the region, for the Bucknell University campus, and for the community at large—making significant differences in the lives of disadvantaged children, adults, and animals, and improving the physical environment of the community. Past service projects have included building an alternative learning lab for the local high school; building a riding trail for physically challenged people; renovating rooms in local YMCAs, headstarts, and homeless shelters; and tutoring special needs children. In total, Management 101 companies have contributed over fifty-five thousand man hours and more than $250,000 to the local community through their service projects.

The Professor

As you have already learned, professors can be an extremely valuable source of information and advice. These individuals, although paid, have basically devoted at least a portion of their lives to helping you get an education. If you think about it, at no other point in your life will you find such a concentrated cluster of professionals, specialists, scholars, researchers, and champions. When I attended Florida A & M there was a slew of lawyers, accountants, doctors, corporate executives, authors, scientists, investment analysts, marketing managers, real estate and insurance agents, and once even a chess champion.

Most professors are a valuable source of information both inside and outside of the classroom. During class, you may learn what's in the textbooks (which by the way, are mostly written by professors). After class, you can learn more about topics covered in the course that can help you tremendously in other areas of your life. Some professors regularly throw out information they think you might need. The professor of my commercial law class, Ronald Jarrett, interspersed his regular lectures with information on tax laws, how to help your parents establish a trust for you, how to write your will, why you need renter's insurance, how to set up your own business, and how to buy real estate. The knowledge I and many of my classmates gained from courses like accounting, investments, commercial law, the legal environment of business, and marketing management have helped us in a number of situations.

Many of the professors will offer their professional services for free either during or after office hours. There were several professors on my campus who offered legal services and conducted seminars free of charge. This sort of advice can have numerous uses in sticky situations. For instance, think about roommates. Roommates can be great! They are friends, cramming buddies, and someone with whom to share expenses and household chores. On the other hand, roommates can steal, lie, escalate a phone bill, and check out on a joint rental lease, leaving you holding the bag. Students left in such a situation, already having little or no cash flow, can seek the advice of the professors on campus willing to help. This usually results in a happy ending—the wronged roommate receiving compensation without paying expensive legal fees.

Professors and instructors help in other ways, too. As a first-semester junior, I wrote a paper for an organizational behavior class. I entitled the paper "Knowledge Creation Within a Company." When my professor for the class, George Neely, returned my paper, I saw not only an A, but also his handwritten, "Come see me!" under my grade. Fearing accusations of plagiarism and collaboration and carefully building a case to prove otherwise, I finally visited his office after several weeks of deliberation. He asked me if I had ever thought about graduate school. I said yes. He then explained several facts and ideas about graduate school, including its importance. He also recommended a program on campus that specialized in preparing students for graduate school and helped the students in the program to find summer research assignments. Even better, before I left his office, he called the director of the McNair Scholars Program and referred me to him.

Professors and instructors are excellent sources for advice and consultations. They can also be wonderful mentors. All you need do is ask. They may say "No," but more often you'll hear "Yes, I'll help." Jordan Scarboro, a student at the University of North Carolina at Chapel Hill concurs. She states: "Always begin talking to your professors early in the class. It's a great way to get to know excellent people who often are at the top of their field. Getting to know your professors will make it easier for you to ask them questions and learn from them. Meeting with them and showing them you are working hard on the class often helps with final grades, especially if you are on the border line. Often they will go out of their way to share special information, whether it is about the class or about really cool campus events. Also, you never know what kind of opportunities will require a recommendation letter or someone to research with. Going to office hours might seem like a pain, but they will pay off in the end."

Jordan also shares this advice about choosing classes and a professor: "Often universities give teaching awards. This is a great way to pick your professors! So many students use web sites so they can learn how easy a class might be, but if someone has earned a teaching award, especially if they are on the list more than once, they are awesome professors! They may not be the easiest, but you will certainly learn TONS!"

5

On Track to Graduate: Time Management and Staying on Schedule

As you begin your college career—or even if you're in the middle of it—I'm sure you have thought about your grade point average (GPA). When I started college I didn't really worry about it, but as sophomore year rolled around, the all-important grade factor began to occupy more and more of my thoughts. Although I am a strong proponent of overall learning and life outside the classroom, I am also an advocate of maintaining a life inside the classroom. It should always be one of your goals to maximize your chance to have an outstanding transcript, as well as have fun and take interesting courses in the process of getting it. Let me explain what I did to fulfill this.

I developed a master plan during my sophomore year that allowed me to make good grades and enjoy myself, especially as a senior, even though I knew I would also be concentrating on admission to graduate school, starting my career, or both. Referencing our course curriculum in the college catalog for my school and major, I listed all the classes I was required to take. I totaled the number of hours required for graduation as a business administration major. I listed the courses and hours I had already taken and compared them to the requirements. Then I plotted my course.

I realized the more hours I took toward graduation requirements as an underclassman (freshman and sophomore years) the more I would be able to relax as an upperclassman. For me, relaxation meant learning about something I've always been interested in rather than getting heavily involved and never surfacing from business school and the world of facts, figures, balance sheets, and the all-important bottom line. I called the classes I chose enhancing classes. Also, I wanted my last days of college to be laid-back as far as graduation was concerned. Even though I knew other activities would be occupying my time—searching for a job, applying to graduate school, and applying for fellowships—I realized quickly that getting required classes out of the way left the field clear for me to focus on the rest of my life. So I budgeted my time.

I knew that to achieve my goal of getting graduation requirements out of the way before senior year, I needed to take at least thirty-six hours per year, eighteen hours per semester. Even though it was at times grueling, by the beginning of my junior year, I was able to decrease my hours to sixteen, then finally fourteen. In my senior year, I took piano lessons (something I had always wanted to do), psychology (another developing interest), golf, Spanish, and several other elective courses.

Maintaining your grades from the time you enter college is important not only for purposes of relaxation, reduced stress, and taking enhancement classes. When you are applying for jobs or graduate school, ideally during the beginning or middle of your last year, your transcript is not going to reflect your final GPA. It will only reflect your grades from the past semester. So unless you are planning to postpone your job or graduate school search until well after you have graduated, you should make sure your grades are up to par before your senior year so you won't be scrambling to bolster your GPA and your ego as admissions officials and recruiters tell you they're not interested.

Time Management

For Hayley Ford, a student at Marquette University, time management was an extremely important factor to help her stay on schedule and maximize her grades. In her words, "I live by my planner. I always write in every major project or test that is due during the course of the semester right away when I receive my syllabi. Then I write in any extracurricular activities or school basketball games or anything that may take up a significant portion of time. I discover any major time conflicts that may arise early, so that I can plan accordingly. Using this method, I have not pulled an all-nighter in two years of college."

Dianna He, a business major and music minor at the University of Pennsylvania agrees, "Time management and setting priorities is key. For many people, it's the first time ever living on their own for an extended period of time. This newfound independence can feel like a blessing, but students must beware of being sucked into the many distractions and methods of procrastination such as Facebook or obsessively checking e-mail."

10 Steps to Managing Your Time

1. Start each day, week, and month with a task list. Cross off tasks as you complete them.

2. Carry an electronic organizer with an audible and/or visible reminder feature for important tasks. Or use your smart phone or tablet alarms and alerts to keep you on track.

3. Post a wall calendar prominently in your room with days clearly marked in red for the completion of assignments and tasks, particularly those that are extremely important.

4. Break complex assignments or projects into smaller bite size segments that are easier to handle. For example, if you have a major research project due in one month, small tasks leading up to the actual project could be discussing the assignment with your professor or teaching assistant, visiting the library and obtaining books on the subject area, or researching relevant web sites.

5. Reward yourself for staying on task. If you complete all or the most important tasks on your list for the day or the week, hang out with friends or go to the next party as your reward.

6. Dedicate blocks of your time. For example, you may decide to devote two hours on Wednesday evening to Principles of Accounting II and one hour afterwards to Physics I.

7. Stop when you get tired of studying or working on an assignment. Schedule a time to return to the assignment later.

When you return, you may have renewed energy and a fresh perspective to help propel you into finishing the assignment.

8. Immediately speak to your professor if you have any upcoming activity, event, or a last minute change in schedule that could hinder you completing an assignment. He or she may be willing to give you additional time.

9. Don't procrastinate. Dive into an assignment as soon as possible. It is much better to start early and complete a dreaded assignment over a period of time which allows you ample opportunity to get help than to avoid an assignment for weeks, throw it together, have limited or no time to get assistance, or worse don't get the assignment done at all.

10. Prioritize! Some assignments may be more important than others. How do you decide? Look at your course syllabus and your class schedule. Assignments that have the greatest impact on your grades should have a higher priority.

Staying on Schedule

Staying on schedule and graduating is the goal of many students. However most don't achieve this goal because they don't start with a plan. When you begin college, you should define your goals for graduation by thinking about the following graduation paths:

- Graduation in four years or less;
- Graduation in four years with internships, study abroad, or other experiences in the summer;
- Graduation in four years or more with internships or co-ops during the regular semester or quarter;
- Graduation undetermined or as long as it takes (perpetual student status).

Once you understand your goal and the financial and emotional consequences associated with your decision, you should learn the courses associated with the major you've chosen and the hours required to complete your degree. Find out when each course you need to take is offered and decide when you plan to take it. To determine when courses may be offered well in advance of the time you need to register, review catalogs and class schedules for several years prior to get an idea. If necessary, contact your advisor or the department associated with the course to determine when a class is typically offered. Once you have a schedule clearly outlining your required courses and the semester or quarter in which you plan to take them, chart your progress at least three times a year. As discussed in chapter one, you should be able to get a degree audit or curriculum check sheet from your advisor or the university web site to help you keep track. Online class schedules, catalogs, and even degree audit sheets may only show the current or immediate past semester or quarter. If that's the case, visit your advisor for information about previous years or the degree audit that applies to you. Or visit the department associated with your major or the course you're interested in taking.

To have fun and get good grades, plan your time *and* your schedule wisely. Know the grades you need to make to achieve the GPA you want. Then go to work! In the words of Zig Ziglar, motivational speaker and founder of the Zig Ziglar Corporation, "You don't pay the price for hard work, you enjoy the benefits. Life is tough, but if you're tough on life, life will be infinitely easier. When you do the things you ought to do when you ought to them, the day will come when you can do the things you want to do when you want to do them."

6

Strategies for Boosting Your GPA and Developing Good Study Habits

Although having the highest grade point average shouldn't be your only focus in college, it should definitely be important to you. Why? Students with higher GPA's often have opportunities for the best internships, scholarships, fellowships, graduate school placements, and job offers. Please remember though, that even if your GPA isn't the greatest, being well-rounded and involved in activities beyond the classroom can overcome a mediocre GPA. Indeed, becoming a well-rounded student is still important even if you have a great GPA, since the best way to differentiate yourself from others in the eyes of prospective employers, fellowship committees, and graduate schools is through your experiences beyond the classroom environment. This book is designed to help you avoid typical college pitfalls and experience all the enrichment activities associated with being a college student. It is your participation in those enrichment activities and your ability to take advantage of all your college life has to offer that will help you become a well-rounded individual with the best opportunities.

Reading this chapter will assist you in discovering strategies for boosting your grades and developing good study habits so you can do well in all of your classes even those that are not your favorites. One of the best ways to boost your GPA is to understand how it is calculated so you will know where you stand in terms of an individual course's impact on your grades. So let's how explore how GPA's are calculated.

Calculating Your GPA

First, obtain the grading scale for your college or university. This will help you determine the weight for each grade you earn in all courses you take while at the school. Is it four points for an A, three points for a B, two points for a C, and zero for an F? Consult your advisor or the college handbook, catalog, or web site to confirm your grading scale. As an example, let's assume your grading scale is similar to the one outlined in this paragraph. Next, determine the number of credit hours associated with each class, lecture, or lab that you're taking. For example, you may have two three-credit-hour courses, and one one-credit-hour course. Perhaps, you earn a C in one class, a B in another class and an A in the lab. The following chart shows how you would calculate your GPA for the semester or quarter that you earned these grades.

Course Name	Course Credit Hours	Your Grade	Grade Weight	Total Class Credit Earned (Grade Weight x Credit Hours)
Chemistry	3	C	2	6
English 101	3	B	3	9
Chemistry Lab	1	A	4	4
	7 Total Credit Hours			19 Total Class Credits
Divide total class credits earned (19) by the number of credit hours attempted (7)			19 ÷ 7 = 2.71 GPA	

You can also use Google (http://www.google.com) to search for, "how do I calculate my GPA?" to find online calculators to help you.

Making the Best Grades

Here are a few strategies you should always keep in mind for getting the most out of your classes and for making the best grades.

- Attend class, be attentive, and ask questions (particularly for class participation credit).
- Learn your professor's hours and use them!
- Develop good study habits.
- Ask for help and extra credit work *before* you need it. Never wait until the day before the exam or the end of the semester to get assistance in a class that is difficult for you. Last minute requests for help usually result in a poor outcome. Erin Husbands, a student at Louisiana State University, offers her advice, "Don't be afraid to ask for help from others in your class or even the professor. Our campus offers free tutoring—it helped me with calculus! . . . Since scholarship is one of their most important aspects, Theta, the sorority I joined, maintained a test notes bank that Theta's donated from previous semesters. This was another wonderful resource I often used. Also, find someone who might have taken the class before and ask for their old notes. You'd be surprised how many people keep old notes."
- Pay attention to your course syllabus. Review it constantly.
- Post all exam dates or approximate dates prominently in a wall calendar, smart phone, tablet or handheld organizer with an automatic reminder.
- Monitor where you are in the course constantly. After your first exam, sit down with your professor to review where you stand in terms of grades for each area outlined in your course syllabus. If you did not do well on the first exam, ask your professor for additional help or study ideas. Though face to face communication is best, at the very least, start an e-mail dialogue with your professor.
- For all reports and papers due for your classes, *always* go the extra mile. Even if not required, always include the following extra touches:

- o Cover page with appropriate graphics that include instructor's name, course title and number, date of submission, your name, and student number unless otherwise instructed.
- o Page numbers.
- o Table of contents.
- o Table of illustrations, tables, and charts.
- o Bibliography or works cited (ask the professor if there is a specific format to follow for a research paper in their class). Include at least five sources for a research paper. When researching use a variety of sources. Do not rely solely on the Internet.
- o If in doubt, ask for an example. Visit your professor and ask to see an example of an A paper received from a former student. Ask what key items contributed to the grade for the paper. Strive to do as well or better on the paper you submit. Even if they don't say it specifically, most professors are impressed by a well-presented paper. This means delivery *and* content matter.

- Never miss the class just before the exam. Many instructors will review for the mid-term or final exam during this period.
- Always take notes in class. Some instructors will structure their exams based partially or entirely on class lectures and examples.
- Even if it seems like the instructor is not following your course materials (books, workbooks, etc.), make sure to keep up with your reading. Some professors will give exams based entirely on the course materials and examples shown in them.
- This is not like high school. You will have no more than one or two exams before your final. This means your opportunities to improve your final grade with a better grade on the next exam are very limited. If you flunk or bomb out on the first exam, your next opportunity may be a midterm, leaving you only one chance to affect your grade with the final exam.

- You should never be surprised by the grade you see on your transcript. You should always communicate with your professor throughout your class term so you know where you stand. You should never think "I'll probably get a B," and then be surprised with a C or D when you get your transcript over Christmas or during the summer.

- Use on-campus study labs. These are usually run by students who excel in that particular study area. However, you should avoid casually formed study groups unless you already have a basic understanding of the subject area. Most study groups are usually organized quickly by a group of students who are shocked at low grades on an exam or difficult homework. In many of these study groups, those who really understand the material are noticeably absent. Unfortunately the lack of understanding means the study time often degenerates into griping about the class or the professor with everyone leaving the group no better off than when they began studying. Avoid this dilemma by first visiting your professor and a study lab for help with areas you don't understand. Then join the study group. Your own understanding and confidence will grow as you explain and review concepts with the rest of the group.

- Never take a wrong answer or failed/poor exam grade and move on. Always visit your professor or a study lab to find out why the answer is wrong or your answer is unclear. Sometimes professors will review answers when the exams are returned during class. Other times they do not. If you don't have a review of exam answers in class, visit your professor for a one-on-one review during office hours. Some professors may give similar questions or review the same concepts on the next exam. This means if you don't understand why you had problems on the first exam, you'll probably do poorly on the next exam if the same concepts are tested.

- If you miss the deadline date for an assignment, don't settle for an F. Ask your professor if you can turn it in late for reduced credit or an automatic one letter grade reduction.

Developing Good Study Habits

In order to make the best grades so you can earn a higher GPA, you need to have good study habits. One of the first things you should do is learn your own study rhythm. How? Consider the following:

- What environment is best for you? Is it in your bed with music blaring, at a quiet library sitting at a table, or lying in the grass at a park?
- What time of day do you get the best ideas or understand the material you read more easily than at any other? Is it late night, early morning, mid-day, or some other time?
- Does being hungry interrupt your thinking? Do you constantly need snacks or does it matter?
- Do you really perform best at the last minute? Many students think they do but quite often when they really assess whether they could have done better, that's not the case.
- Do you understand concepts better in a group setting or on your own?
- Do you retain information best by listening or reading? For example, Erin Husbands, the student mentioned earlier in the chapter, started recording her classes. She says, "I am a visual person. However, when the professor said something I didn't quite grasp, I started recording the classes. I made CD's and listened to them in the car. I also advise reviewing what you've learned that day, while things are new."

Once you have considered the answers to all of the above, think about the best and worst grades you've earned on exams, papers, and quizzes. Ponder how you habitually study for an exam or prepare research papers. Try to establish a pattern between the best grades you've received and the study methods you used to earn those grades. When you begin to see a link between your best grades and the study habits that led to earning them, you've discovered the study rhythm you should use for the optimal results. If you haven't earned any grades you would consider good, use the methods discussed in this chapter to help you improve. Then, work on determining your study rhythm.

How do you know what and how to study? The following is a list of activities to help you determine the answer.

- Take good class notes and review them before the exam. Also review important or highlighted concepts in your textbook.

- Visit your professor or graduate teaching assistant and ask for study advice to help you prepare for exams, papers, and other important evaluations.

- After each exam you take, review your mistakes in a study lab or with the course's teaching assistant or professor during office hours. You may see the same or a similar question again.

- You should always get prepared for an exam or a research paper well ahead of time. Prepare a study plan with progress dates leading up to an exam or due date for a research paper or essay.

- Study in a location that will have the least amount of distractions. Stephen Schorn, a student at the University of Virginia suggests, "If you have time between classes, go to the library to study or do work. If you go back to your dorm, you may get caught talking to someone online, watching TV, or taking a nap—secluding yourself from any distractions will force you to do work you otherwise may not do."

7

Getting Internships, Cooperative Education and Other Learning Experiences Beyond the Classroom

Have you ever wanted to visit another part of the country, meet new people, escape from the humdrum of the classroom, or earn a few extra dollars working in a field that interests you? If you answered yes to any of these questions, then an applied learning program is definitely the route for you. Applied learning, an educational tool that has been in existence for over half a century, can be found in several different forms. It includes cooperative education (co-ops), internships, experiential learning, apprenticeships, and occupational learning. These are all based on experience and learning that occurs almost entirely beyond the classroom. Applied learning also allows self-assessment, the clarification of goals, and the identification of entry barriers within a particular field.

The benefits of applied learning are recognized at most post-secondary institutions. The University of Cincinnati was one of the first institutions to use applied learning as an educational tool, followed by Antioch University, Georgia Institute of Technology, and Drexel University. Currently, almost every post-secondary institution has some form of or access to applied learning programs. Let's consider some of the benefits of applied learning.

Benefits

- *Work experience*–An internship, cooperative education program (co-op), or other form of applied learning can provide you with actual work experience in the field in which you are interested. When you participate in an internship, a potential employer can assess your work habits to see if they will fit within that organization. In turn, you can assess yourself to decide if you actually want to work in that particular field. Janel Janiczek, a graduate from the University of Pittsburgh, agrees. She says: "Work experiences are invaluable because they give you real world experiences that cannot be taught in a classroom. You learn lessons about dealing with people and how to make the most of your time and talents."

- *Money*–Many internships and cooperative programs are paid. Some companies and organizations may take care of living expenses as well. Corporate internships usually pay approximately 75 to 85 percent of the monthly salary paid to full-time employees in a particular field. Nonprofit and government organizations usually pay considerably less than their corporate counterparts and may pay nothing. Your compensation will depend on the organization, your field of interest, and the location of the internship. Regardless of whether the internship does or does not pay, it is a valuable source of work experience and may also have many of the other benefits listed here.

- *Contacts*–As you get to know individuals within an organization you begin to develop contacts. You can refer to your contacts in the future to gain job-related or other types of information. For example, John Doe at XYZ Company may keep you in mind or know of a job opening at XYZ that would be perfect for you when you graduate. When I was an intern at EDS in Belgium, I needed some information from a written document I had completed the previous year at EDS in Raleigh, North Carolina. I called one of my contacts at the Raleigh office and she sent that document overnight, as well as others that were helpful. Staying in touch with your business contacts has become even easier with social media platforms such as LinkedIn. Creating a LinkedIn profile (http://www.linkedin.com) is an essential tool for maintaining your business relationships.

- *References*–In many applied programs you have several supervisors and can use other coworkers as mentors. These individuals can serve as excellent references since they have firsthand knowledge of your abilities. These references can be used not only for employment purposes but also when applying for graduate school, scholarships, fellowships, and merit awards.

- *Travel*–Some internships and co-op programs offer opportunities to travel. For example, as a sales intern for Armstrong, I went to New York, New Jersey, Maryland, and the District of Columbia. Travel opportunities will depend on the organization, the job itself, and the primary location of the internship.

- *Mentor*–Many prominent and successful men and women have attributed at least part of their success to the presence of a mentor in their lives. Mentors are people who can see the promise in a young individual, especially one in their career field. As a mentor they take the time to steer that individual in the right direction, give insight into a particular field, and offer tips on avoiding standard pitfalls. Essentially, they aid others by relating the knowledge they have gained through life in general and through working for a number of years in a particular career. Internships and co-ops are excellent opportunities to find and develop lasting relationships with people who can help shape your life and career.

- *Technical skills*–As an intern or co-op, you may be taught certain skills in workshops, training sessions, webinars, or seminars in order to do your job effectively. These skills may be particular to an industry or they may be applicable to other jobs or activities you decide to undertake. For example, in my first internship with EDS in Raleigh, North Carolina, I learned the difference between technical writing and creative writing. I also learned how to use MacDraw and Microsoft Word software applications on Apple computers and operating systems. In addition, we worked entirely in teams, and at the end of my internship I functioned as a manager of one of the teams. During my internship with Armstrong World Industries, interns participated in several seminars on topics including selling skills, goal setting, presentation skills, relationship strategies, and writing skills. All of these seminars contributed significantly to my development as an individual, but all are relevant to any job or activity, not just an Armstrong marketing representative. In sum, I developed the following skills from my internships: technical writing, managing and working with the team-based approach, and computer skills and proficiency with MacDraw and Microsoft Word on a new (to me) but widely used hardware system. I also acquired other, less obvious skills, such as effective time management because we worked under deadline almost entirely, as well as how to manage stress in our deadline-oriented environment.

- *Enhanced knowledge through application*–Application of the knowledge you gain in class can solidify and enhance what you have learned. For example, I did not fully understand the concepts in my production management class. Even though I did well, just-in-time management and other expediting functions were memory definitions for me, not actual applications. However, because of my internship with Armstrong, I understand not only the definitions but also how these concepts might be needed in the business world. In addition, I was able to present my own examples in class for discussion purposes.

- *Decision tool*–Your internship or other applied learning experience is always a decision tool. Even if you are interning in a field totally unrelated to your major, the internship can help you decide whether you like the field enough to abandon your current major and try another, whether you want to double major, or whether you want to develop this new interest into a minor. When making a career choice later, your internship or applied learning experience will also aid you in making difficult choices, including multiple job offers, graduate school admissions, or fellowships.

- *Possible job offer after graduation*–Although for most a job offer is a possibility and not a guarantee, if you do an excellent job as an intern or co-op, you have a good chance of being offered a job after you graduate. The company gains by having much of your training already done when you were an intern or co-op; you gain by having a possible job offer in your back pocket.

- ***Books***–Books are sometimes given to interns to further their development in a particular area. These books may be especially helpful for research in a later required class.
- ***Scholarship aid***–Some companies and organizations that sponsor internships offer scholarships to those who are selected to participate.
- ***Friends***–During your internship or co-op program you will probably hang out with other interns, co-ops, or employees at the company or organization in which you work. In the midst of the fun, laughter, and work, some of these may become lasting friendships. These friends could become valuable contacts for you in the future, particularly if they work for the organization in which you interned or for another organization that also interests you. Make sure to connect with them on Facebook, LinkedIn or Twitter.

Experiential or Occupational Learning

Experiential or occupational learning is learning based on experience. Someone who has learned experientially or occupationally has already started his or her career or spent considerable time working in a particular area. For example, if you have worked for several years as a sales representative and then decide to go back to college to complete your degree in marketing, you may be eligible for academic credit for the years you spent on the job, depending on the college. The credit would be based on your past experiences and the knowledge you gained in your occupation. In some cases, internships and other applied learning programs are also considered experiential learning and are available for credit.

Internships

Internships are valuable experiences for all college students, for those who may need a little direction in deciding on a career, as well as for those who hope to get a job in a tight job market. Even if the job market is not tight, internships and other job experiences can give you an edge over other job seekers and may result in multiple job offers when you graduate. Internships can be structured or unstructured forms of applied learning. They can be paid or unpaid. Internships can coincide with your academic program of study or be in another area, and can last from one month to several months. They are available in a range of organizations and locations. For example, an internship can be in a corporation, a medical laboratory, a newspaper, a department store, or on an archaeological site.

Through an internship you can strengthen your knowledge base and also determine whether your major and field of interest are right for you. An internship can result in your meeting people who could be extremely helpful and resourceful contacts for you in the future, and it allows you to apply the knowledge you have learned from textbooks and professors to the real world.

An internship is also a good start in making the transition from insulated college life to the hectic environment beyond the college campus. It may involve travel all over the United States or even the world. For Hodari Brown, a Tennessee State University student, the internship experience was especially rewarding. Hodari explains: "My internships in particular have been beneficial to my major and future career goals. In terms of working on senatorial and presidential campaigns, which have opened the door to other job opportunities and work experiences … I have been able to meet several influential individuals such as Harold Ford Jr., President Barack Obama (before he was elected), Hillary Clinton, John Edwards, President George W. Bush, and others through my internships …"

Before my internship with Armstrong World Industries, a manufacturing company based in Lancaster, Pennsylvania, I knew nothing of the sales and marketing field. Previously, the idea of selling anyone anything was extremely distasteful to me. When I read Armstrong's job description for a summer internship as a marketing representative, my mind focused on two words, "sales territory," immediately conjuring up images of selling doughnuts, candy, and other knickknacks for numerous school projects and clubs as a child.

I remember the horrors of having people give me the sweet and often false response "We already have" to my childish sales pitch "Would you like to buy some of our ..." I also remember our house being filled with merchandise that my mother bought to keep me from suffering repeated rejections and further injury to my pint-sized ego. Needless to say, a sales internship did not appeal to me. However, because I liked the company overall and especially the recruiters, I decided to give it a try. It was one of the best decisions I have ever made—I discovered I love sales and marketing!

My childhood fears have been replaced by an adult reality. Had I never experienced the Armstrong sales internship, my career options would have been limited, mainly due to my own ignorance. Now I know the field of sales and marketing is highly interesting, charged with responsibility, and can be extremely profitable. Not only that, many jobs in this field are consulting-oriented, rather than make-the-sale-no-matter-what-oriented. Through this experience I learned if a customer has a need or a problem and you as the sales representative demonstrate the knowledge, experience, and willingness to satisfy his or her needs, while providing an effective solution for the problem, the sale will follow. Until my internship with Armstrong, I never knew that. Since that summer, I developed a fascination with this field and even took courses to further my interest.

For most college graduates relevant work experience is a necessity for landing at least one job offer. Nowadays most employers want to see students who not only have good GPAs, but also potential. They want students who can walk into a job and hit the ground running. Because most companies are rightsizing, streamlining, and downsizing, students are under increasing pressure to show their talents and value to potential employers. One of the best ways to do so is to have had at least one internship in the field you plan to enter or even another unrelated but complementary field. But internships can only be valuable in this way if you know how to sell the experience you have gained from them and show your resulting growth as an individual. If you have had an internship, highlight the job duties and responsibilities it carried on your résumé in the work experience section as shown in the résumés in chapter one. You also need to be prepared to emphasize your internship during interviews with potential employers. If it's on your résumé, they will probably ask about it. When you talk about the internship, be certain to show confidence and assert the effort and knowledge you contributed and gained from the internship and make sure your experience is included in your LinkedIn profile.

Many career centers at universities and colleges can help students find internships with major corporations, public service agencies, the government, or other profit or nonprofit entities. Some also sponsor internship expositions in which hundreds of these organizations participate. And many have online job postings from prospective employers.

Remember, the very least an internship can do is give you some work experience. In today's job society experience matters a lot. Use your time at college wisely and get the most for your money by getting at least one internship. You may find that it will change your life. You can learn more about internship opportunities by visiting the career center at your college or university, or by directly contacting the organizations included at the end of this chapter in the abbreviated listing of organizations offering internships, cooperative education programs, or summer jobs by industry. You can also read the *Vault Guide to Top Internships* (http:///www.vault.com), or use the following web sites for more information about internship programs.

- YouTern—http://www.youtern
- InternMatch—http://www.internmatch.com
- CollegeRecruiter—http://www.collegerecruiter.com
- Internships.com—http://www.internships.com
- InternJobs.com—http://www.internjobs.com
- MonsterTRAK—http://www.monstertrak.monster.com /msnintern

Using the Internet, you can easily determine if a company or organization you're interested in offers internships. Visit the company or organization web site and search the careers or jobs section. In this section you can usually narrow your search even further by looking for student programs or internships. As an example, I visited Dell's web site, http://www.dell.com. I went to their site map, clicked on *About Dell*, then selected *Careers*. Next, I clicked *Internships* where I was able to find information about their internship program. For other companies you can also visit the *About Us* or *Corporate* pages of their web sites to begin your search for internship opportunities. If you can't find information on a company's web site, call the company and request their university relations, college relations, or human resources department. You can also use an advanced Internet search to determine if a company has an internship program. To conduct an advanced search, go to a search engine such as Google or Yahoo! On the main tool bar at the top of the page, look for *More*. In the drop down box, choose *Advanced Search*. You should see options on the page that appear similar to the image below. This search was done specifically to determine if Disney had an internship program. However you could use the advanced search to find internships or students programs with any company or organization that makes information about their programs publicly available on the Internet.

Advanced Search		
Find Results	all of these words	
	the exact phrase	internship
	any of these words	Disney
	none of these words	

Cooperative Education

Cooperative education combines formal academic training with actual work experience–either part-time or full-time work for which a student is usually paid–in a structured course of study. This type of program can last from several months to a year. Any of the following plans may be used for cooperative education (co-ops).

- Parallel–part time work and part-time study;

- Extended day–full time study and part-time work or full-time work and part-time study;
- Alternating–full-time work and full-time study in alternating patterns–for example, you can work one semester or quarter and study in school for the next semester or quarter.

Part-time study is a course load of less than 12 hours per semester or less than 9 hours per quarter.

You can also conduct an advanced Internet search for cooperative education programs in a specific area, with specific colleges and universities, or with certain employers. See the section on internships earlier in this chapter for more information about conducting an advanced Internet search.

Visit your career center to get more information about cooperative programs at your institution. Your college or university may also have a separate department to handle co-op programs. Refer to the end of the chapter for an abbreviated listing of organizations that may offer co-op programs.

Both internships and cooperative education can be essential to helping you obtain the best and even multiple job offers when you are ready to graduate from college. According to a recent survey conducted by the National Association of Colleges and Employers (NACE – http://www.naceweb.org), many employers are planning to fill more than 40 percent of their entry level positions with college graduates from their own internship and co-op programs.

STUDENT HIGHLIGHT

Applied learning in the form of cooperative education was a major decision tool and a very good source of both money and technical skills for Jany Kay Allen, a graduate of the Georgia Institute of Technology in Atlanta. Through Georgia Tech's cooperative education program, Jany was involved in a co-op program with a small engineering consulting firm in Atlanta. She began the program in the fall of her sophomore year and completed it in the spring two and a half years later.

During her co-op term, Jany was involved in several in-house training programs, one of which helped to hone her technical writing skills, a key advantage in the consulting industry. She says she became "very knowledgeable about several software programs, which have definitely helped me in school." She also examined her company's affirmative action policies in a critical analysis speech prepared for a public speaking class. Jany explained: "At the time the company was not affected by affirmative action policies. As a result, the company had only two professional women, no African Americans, and no other minority groups on the payroll. I gave my speech as if I were talking to the company at an employee meeting."

For Jany, one of the biggest advantages from her co-op experience was the salary, which helped tremendously with tuition costs. Although her internship experience wasn't all roses, her co-op experience did give her a good idea of how to approach future employment. Jany stated, "I enjoyed my co-op experience very much, but I knew afterwards that I did not want to work for a small company because I saw tremendous value in wellness programs, company outings, and team building. I do believe I will stay in consulting."

Summer Jobs/Programs

Some corporations offer jobs to college students for the summer only. Internships and summer jobs are similar. The major difference between a summer job and an internship is that almost all summer jobs are paid positions, whereas many internships are not. In addition, internships can occur at any time of the school year, rather than just in the summer, as long as it is agreed upon by you and the organization or corporation for which you will be working. Also, most internships are structured programs designed to provide the most beneficial learning experience possible for you as the intern and also for the corporation, should they decide to hire you for a permanent job. Lastly, for many internships you can get academic credit, whereas for most summer jobs you cannot.

However, a summer job can still be a tremendous learning experience and it carries many of the same benefits as those outlined for internships and co-ops. In some cases, you may be able to get a summer job transferred into an internship and receive academic credit for it. Consult someone in your major department or the career center first to learn whether this is an option. Review the organizations at the end of this chapter for possible summer job opportunities.

Research Programs

If you really want to explore your major and all of its possibilities, getting involved in a research program is an excellent way to do so. Most research programs are structured to allow you to conduct your research independently, as part of a team, or with a professor or other faculty member. Research programs allow you to delve deeper into a particular field. You might even uncover incredible information.

For example, as a part of a research effort, several math majors at Florida Agricultural and Mechanical University constructed mathematical models as a solution to cancer. Who would think of math as a solution for helping to find a cure for a disease? If you get involved in a research program, you might think of math, science, sociology, or statistics in a variety of different ways only a serious researcher would know about.

AT & T Labs Research is one example of a company that may offer summer research opportunities for students. Visit http://www.research.att.com for more information. You may also want to contact their university relations department and ask for the special programs manager to inquire about summer research opportunities. And don't forget to contact *your* university career center to get more information about summer research programs to which they can direct you.

STUDENT HIGHLIGHT

Angela Grant, formerly a Ph.D. candidate at the University of Michigan and later a professor at Northwestern University (she received her Ph. D from the University of Maryland), believed that her research experience at the University of Illinois in Champaign was one of the key factors in her acceptance in the University of Michigan graduate program and her winning a prestigious National Science Foundation Fellowship. Angela had taken advantage of a summer research opportunity program during her undergraduate college career. Not only did she have an interesting summer exploring the vast world of pure mathematics at its best and worst, but her research experience also helped to propel her toward earning her doctorate in math and ultimately a position as assistant professor for a major university.

In her senior year at the University of North Carolina at Chapel Hill Jordan Scarboro stated, "Research is a great way to get involved on campus with professors and other students. My current research project is UNC ACCESS, which studies handicap accessibility on higher education campuses. The project has been going on for a few years now and the final results are in! The great thing about the project is the travel to many statewide and national conferences, such as *Research in the Capital* and the Association on Higher Education and Disability (AHEAD) annual conference.

Jordan also indicated, "*Research in the Capital* was a poster session where 100 projects were selected from around the state to be presented to the North Carolina legislature. As students we realized being involved in the poster session could really help legislators to recognize major projects in which college students were involved, particularly since their understanding could positively affect their votes on school funding."

Jordan continued, "National conferences for research are also fun! They are great ways to train yourself for the workplace and they look wonderful on a résumés! Often schools will pay for your travel and conference expenses."

Directed Individual Study (DIS)

Directed individual study (DIS) is academic course work usually supervised by an advisor from your department. You may design the course under the supervision of your advisor, and decide your own pace. In many cases, the advisor may administer tests or require a written paper, presentation, research project, or all three upon completion of your studies. The period of study usually lasts the length of a regular class term. You won't have classes to attend, but you may have periodic meetings with your advisor to discuss your progress. For DIS you could receive anywhere from one to six credit hours, possibly more. Credit depends on your advisor, the department, and the quantity and quality of work you do. This program may not be available everywhere.

A reading course is also an option if you are interested in taking a course that is generally not offered by your university, not available during the time you need to take it, or the subject area does not have enough interested students to warrant being offered by the university. Check with your advisor for more information.

Internships, Co-ops, & Summer Job Opportunities by Industry

This is an abbreviated listing. Other opportunities may be available.

Many of the companies listed below are on various social media platforms. When visiting the web sites, get connected with them through Facebook, Twitter and LinkedIn if the option is available.

NON-PROFIT

American Diabetes Association
1701 North Beauregard Street

Alexandria, VA 22311
Phone: (800) 342-2383
Web Site: http://www.diabetes.org (see careers > intern opportunities)

American Red Cross National Headquarters
Summer Internship Program
2025 E Street NW
Washington, DC 20006
Phone: (202) 303-4498
E-mail: internships @redcross.org
Web Site: http://www.redcross.org (see career opportunities > summer internship program)

United Way of America
The United Way Summer Associate Program
701 North Fairfax Street
Alexandria, VA 22314
Phone: (703) 836-7100
Web Site: http://www.unitedway.org (see jobs > summer associate program)

GOVERNMENT

Central Intelligence Agency
Undergraduate Internship Program
Undergraduate Co-Op Program
Office of Public Affairs
Washington, DC 20505
Phone: (703) 482-0623
Web Site: http://www.cia.gov (see careers and internships > student opportunities)

National Aeronautics and Space Administration (NASA)
Headquarters

Office of Education
300 E Street SW
Washington, DC 20024
Phone: (202) 358-0000
Web Site: https://intern.nasa.gov

Naval Facilities Engineering Command (NAVFAC)
1322 Patterson Ave. SE, Suite 1000
Washington Navy Yard
Washington, DC 20374-5065
Web Site: https://portal.navfac.navy.mil (see employment >
internships)

U.S. Department of State
Student Internship Programs
2201 C Street NW
Washington, DC 20520
Phone: Pathways Internship Program: 1-866-300-7419 (202);
Unpaid Student Internship Program: (202) 261-8888
E-mail: Pathways Internship Program: HRSC@state.gov; Unpaid
Student Internship Program: StudentProgramsSecurity@state.gov
Web Site: http://careers.state.gov/students or www.state.gov (see
youth & education > student career programs)

White House Internship Program
The White House
Intern Coordinator
1600 Pennsylvania Avenue NW
Washington, DC 20500
Phone: (202) 456-1414
E-mail: intern_application@whitehouse.gov
Web Site: http://www.whitehouse.gov/about/internships or
http://www.whitehouse.gov (see the white house > white house
internships)

FINANCE

Deloitte Corporate Finance LLC
30 Rockefeller Plaza
New York, NY
10112-0015
Phone: (212) 492-4000
Web Site: http://careers.deloitte.com/students_internships.aspx or http://www.deloitte.com (see careers > students)

Goldman Sachs
200 West Street
New York, New York, 10282
Phone: (212) 902-1000
Web Site: http://www2.goldmansachs.com/careers/career_paths/in dex.html or http://www.goldmansachs.com (see careers > our programs or search for internships)

PricewaterhouseCoopers (PwC)
300 Madison Avenue, 24th Floor
New York, NY 10036
Phone: (646) 471 4000
Web Site: http://www.pwc.com (see careers > United States > campus candidates > student programs > internships)

UBS
1285 Avenue of the Americas
New York, NY 10019
Phone: 212-713-2000
Web Site: http://www.ubs.com (see careers > graduates and interns)

RETAIL

Sears Holding Corporation
Internship Undergraduate Programs

3333 Beverly Road
Hoffman Estates, IL 60179
Phone: (847) 286-2500
Web Site: www.searsholdings.com/careers or www.searsholdings.com
(see careers > collegiate programs)

Target Corporation
1000 Nicollet Mall
Minneapolis, MN 55403
Phone: (612) 304-6073
Web Site: https://corporate.target.com/careers (see > find internships
and careers for students)

The TJX Companies Inc.
770 Cochituate Road
Framingham, MA 01701
Phone: (508) 390-1000
Web Site: http://www.tjx.com/careers (see college recruitment >
internships)

MEDIA/ARTS/ENTERTAINMENT

Academy of Television Arts & Sciences Foundation
5220 Lankershim Blvd.
North Hollywood, CA 91601-3109
Phone: (818) 754-2800
Web Site: http://www.emmysfoundation.org (see student internship
program)

American Repertory Theatre and Institute for Advanced Theatre
Training
Internship Director
64 Brattle Street
Cambridge, MA 02138
Phone: (617) 495-2666

Web Site: http://www.americanrepertorytheater.org/intern

National Football League (NFL)
280 Park Avenue
New York, NY 10017
Phone: (212) 450-2000
Web Site: http://www.nfl.com (see league employment for
internships specifically with the NFL and team employment for
internships with various teams)

NBC Universal
E-mail: nbcucareers@nbcuni.com
Web Site: http://www.nbcunicareers.com/internships

The John F. Kennedy Center for the Performing Arts
Kennedy Center Arts Management
2700 F Street, NW
Washington, DC 20566
Phone: (202) 416-8874
E-mail: internship@kennedy-center.org
Web Site: http://www.kennedy-center.org/education/arts
management/internships/ or www.kennedycenter.com (see
internship)

Walt Disney Co.
500 South Buena Vista Street
Burbank, CA 91521
Phone: (818) 560-1000
Web Site: www.disney.com (see internship) or
www.disneycareers.com (see students recent grads)

Wolf Trap Foundation for the Performing Arts
Internship Program
1645 Trap Road
Vienna, VA 22182

Phone: (703) 937-6304 or 1 (800) 404-8461
Email: internships@wolftrap.org
Web Site: http://www.wolftrap.org/Education/Internships_for_
College_Students.aspx or http://www.wolftrap.org (see internships)

Viacom Inc.
1515 Broadway
New York, NY 10036
Phone: (212) 258-6000
Web Site: http://www.viacom.com (see careers > internships)

TECHNOLOGY

Apple Inc.
1 Infinite Loop
Cupertino, CA 95014
Phone: (408) 996-1010
Web Site: http://www.apple.com/jobs/us/students.html or
http://www.apple.com (see job opportunities > students > internship)

Cisco Systems, Inc.
Corporate Headquarters
170 West Tasman Dr.
San Jose, CA 95134
Web Site: http://www.cisco.com (see career opportunities > graduate
jobs and internships)

Intel Corporation
2200 Mission College Blvd.
Santa Clara, CA 95054-1549
Phone: (408) 765-8080
Web Site: http://www.intel.com (see jobs > student centers)

International Business Machines Corporation (IBM)
1 New Orchard Road

Armonk, NY 10504
Phone: (914) 499-1900
Web Site: http://www.ibm.com/careers (see university students >
targeted internship programs)

Microsoft Corporation
One Microsoft Way
Redmond, WA 98052-6399
Phone: (425) 882-8080
Web Site: http://www.microsoft.com (see careers > internships)

CONSUMER/BUSINESS PRODUCTS

CVS Caremark Corporation
Corporate Headquarters
One CVS Drive
Woonsocket, RI 02895
Phone: (401) 765-1500
Web Site: http://careers.cvscaremark.com/(see who we hire >
internships)

SC Johnson
1525 Howe Street
Racine, WI 53403
Phone: (262) 260-2154
Web Site: http://www.scjohnson.com/en/Careers (search for
internships)

E. I. du Pont de Nemours & Co.
1007 N Market St
Wilmington, DE 19898
Phone: (302) 774-1000
Web Site: http://www.dupont.com (see university recruiting >
internships and co-ops)

WR Grace & Co.
7500 Grace Drive
Columbia, MD 21044
Phone: (410) 531-4000
Web Site: http://www.grace.com (see careers > students)

Lockheed Martin Corporation
6801 Rockledge Drive
Bethesda, MD 20817
Phone: (301) 897-6000
Web Site: http://www.lockheedjobs.com (see college students > internships) or http://www.lockheedmartin.com

Merck & Co. Inc.
One Merck Drive
Whitehouse Station, NJ 08889-0100
Phone: (908) 423-1000
Web Site: http://www.merck.com/careers/university/internships. html

CONSUMER/BUSINESS SERVICES

EMC Corporation
176 South Street
Hopkinton, MA 01748
Phone: (508) 435-1000
Web Site: http://www.emc.com/careers/index.htm (see students and recent grads)

Enterprise Rent-A-Car
600 Corporate Park Drive
St. Louis, MO 63105
Phone: (314) 512-5000
Web Site: http://www.enterprise.com (see careers > opportunities > internships) or http://www.erac.com

Exelon Corporation
10 South Dearborn Street, 48th Floor
Chicago, IL 60680-5398
Phone: (800) 483-3220
Web Site: http://www.exeloncorp.com/peopleandculture/opport
unities/Pages/students.aspx or http://www.exeloncorp.com (see
careers)

The Northwestern Mutual Life Insurance Company
720 East Wisconsin Avenue
Milwaukee, WI 53202-4797
Phone: (414) 271-1444
Web Site: http://www.northwesternmutual.com (see career
opportunities > financial representative internship)

HOSPITALITY

Marriott International Inc.
10400 Fernwood Rd
Bethesda, MD 20817
Phone: (301) 380-3000
Web Site: http://www.marriott.com (see careers > student or recent
graduate > internships)

The Venetian Resort Hotel Casino
3355 Las Vegas Blvd. South
Las Vegas, NV 89109
Phone: (414) JOBS (5627)
E-mail: employment@venetian.com
Web Site: http://www.venetian.com (see careers >summer
internships)

8

The International Experience

If you want to escape the traditional confines of your university or college and further your education and experience in an international setting, then working or studying abroad may be just the thing for you. To many graduate schools and prospective employers, global experience is a key factor in acceptance or getting the job. So have a little fun, experience a new culture, and enlighten your mind with the traditions and customs of a different country. Go abroad! Although you may have visited a foreign country before, living, working, or studying in one is a completely different experience.

Going Abroad – The Basics

Going to live and work abroad is an undertaking that requires careful planning. There are many books and web sites dedicated solely to the experience of working and studying abroad, so I will not go too deeply into the planning process. However, I will provide you with a little background information and tell you about my own experiences abroad.

Work and study abroad programs are sponsored by universities here in the United States and by a consortium of universities that have formed an independent organization for the specific purpose of fostering international student endeavors. Programs are also sponsored by independent organizations that have no ties to a specific university, college, or consortium in the United States.

The Council on International Educational Exchange (CIEE), with offices worldwide, is one of the largest and most comprehensive organizations currently offering assistance to students who wish to travel, work, or study abroad. CIEE has many divisions offering numerous services. For example, CIEE (http://www.ciee.org or (800) 40-STUDY) maintains the information and the student services department, which answers inquiries from students interested in going abroad. When I went to Brussels, Belgium, as an intern for Electronic Data Systems (EDS), the company and its expatriate administration used the services of CIEE to assist me.

CIEE also helps students by providing information about helpful resources that can be used to make the study or work abroad experience a safe and enriching experience. One of the most important resources I found through CIEE was the need for a student identity card. The idea of a student travel card came from the International Student Travel Confederation (http://www.aboutistc. org), which is made up of student travel organizations in various countries. ISTC offers the International Student Identity Card (http://www.isic.org) and other cards for those under twenty-six and is the most widely recognized international student card. Depending upon where you're located, the card may offer discounts at theaters, movies, accommodations, museums, restaurants, train stations, and so on. In addition to these discounts and others related to travel, the card also provides a twenty-four-hour emergency hotline and insurance. I found it to be well worth the fee.

If you are looking for travel insurance in addition to the types of services offered by the ISTC identity card, consider the iNext (http://www.inext.com) card. ISTC can also assist with making discounted and very flexible travel arrangements through their student travel department (Student Air Travel Association – SATA).

Before I went to Brussels, I also made use of the free student travel catalogs and brochures published by CIEE. The publications and resources available through CIEE (most of which are now online through their online orientation) are full of useful information including articles, the application process for student travel cards and various international programs, tips on what to bring, and a host of information designed to help students make their travel a worthwhile and exhilarating experience. You can also find other guides to help you with planning your international experience at http://www. independenttraveler.com.

I used or inquired about most of the travel services offered through CIEE and ISTC at one time or another while I prepared for my internship in Brussels. I found the airfares varied. Although my airfare was covered by EDS, the company I interned with, my best friend was planning to visit and needed the lowest possible airfare. I encouraged her to get an International Student Exchange Identity Card (ISE Card) as I had, so we could take advantage of special student discounts. You can get more information about this card at http://www.isecard.com/products. ISTC also has student identity cards. In some cases you may be able to get the student discount for those under 26 by showing valid identification even without a special card. We both shopped around for the best airfares. ISIC also has cards available at (http://www.isic.org). Even though we thought airfares offered by the student travel offices would be the least expensive, we actually found some flights directly through the airlines with lower fares.

We later traveled with another friend to various cities throughout Europe. Although the Eurail passes offered by the student travel offices were a great deal, all three of us found that, armed with the youth international identity card, we could get super train fares at the spur of the moment to any city. It was wonderful and–most important, from our college student perspective–it was cheap! However if you want the flexibility to change your travel plans at a moment's notice, the deals offered through the student travel departments with ISTC may be your best bet. You can also contact STA Travel at http://www.statravel.com or (800) 781-4040 for more student travel discounts.

For reviews of various study, work, volunteer and teach abroad programs, visit http://www.gooverseas.com. This site has postings of reviews from individuals throughout the world who've been involved in international work, teach, volunteer and study abroad programs.

Overseas Job Opportunities

Students interested in working abroad need a work permit or work visa to officially enter and work in another country. Organizations involved in arranging study, work, volunteer and teach abroad programs should obtain these documents for you or help you to obtain them.

The following are several of the many different opportunities for working abroad. Most of these programs mentioned below can also be found on most social media platforms such as Facebook, Twitter, Pinterest and YouTube. Make sure to get connected with them so you can learn as much about the program by reading the posts, looking at pictures and perusing other interesting information.

The Au Pair

Would you like to stay in someone's home and be an au pair? Au pairs are usually young single women interested in learning the language and culture of a particular country. By arrangement, the student lives with and cares for the children of a host family. On my trip to Belgium, my seatmate on the airplane was a Belgian au pair returning from Los Angeles. She shared with me her views on our country and what she missed most about her own during her stay in America. She said she missed the Belgian bread the most. Ours was too soft! Besides the bread, she told me she had improved her English a lot, and she liked to see the movie theater and concerts. She also loved our libraries.

Au pairs are expected to work from thirty to forty-five hours per week caring for the children of the host family. This could include playing with the children, taking the children to and from school, or helping with their homework. If you are interested in becoming an au pair, contact The International Au Pair Association (IAPA) at http://www.iapa.org for a list of organizations to contact.

International Internship

An international internship offers you the opportunity to gain valuable experience and enhance your awareness of the global environment. An international internship can be paid or unpaid. For information about international internships, explore http://www.internabroad.com. This site maintains a pretty good list of opportunities to work abroad. Also visit http://www.culturalvistas.org for more information about international work opportunities.

The International Association of Students in Economics and Commerce (AIESEC) offers full-time students at college and universities worldwide the opportunity to gain hands-on management and leadership skills with a global perspective. Students can participate in international conferences or work abroad in an internship exchange program in a variety of business-related fields. For more information, contact AIESEC United States, 11 Hanover Square, Suite 1700, Manhattan, New York, NY 10005, phone: (212) 757-3774, web site: http://www.aiesecus.org.

Practical on-the-job experience for college and university students is one of the services offered by the International Association for the Exchange of Students for Technical Experience (IAESTE). Students of architecture, computer science, engineering, mathematics, and other related technical fields have the opportunity to gain experience in more than fifty countries. For further information, contact IAESTE United States through Cultural Vistas, 440 Park Avenue South, Second Floor, New York, NY 10016, phone: (212) 497-3500, e-mail: iaeste@culturalvistas.org, web site: http://www.iaesteunitedstates.org.

Volunteer Abroad–Work Camps, Farming, Field Research

If you are interested in volunteering your services abroad, the International Volunteer Programs Association (IVPA) provides information to guide and inform students about available opportunities. For more information, visit http://www.volunteer international.org or e-mail: info@volunteerinternational.org.

You can also contact the Institute for Field Research Expeditions (IFRE) at 3131 McKinney Avenue Suite # 600, Dallas, TX, 75204, Phone: 1-800-675-2504 or (214) 390-7947 (overseas callers), e-mail: info@ifrevolunteers.org or web site: http://

www.ifrevolunteers.org. Currently, IFRE offers volunteer abroad programs in Nepal, India, Sri Lanka, China, Thailand, Peru, Costa Rica, Ghana, Kenya, South Africa, and Tanzania.

Be aware that many volunteer abroad programs have program fees which can be cost prohibitive for a student. Research the programs first. Also ask a professor or department head for your major or minor course of study about cost-effective programs. They may know about programs requiring little or no money from students for volunteer abroad program fees. You can also contact local churches in your area to learn about any upcoming mission trips you can join. For many of the mission trips, your costs may include only travel and lodging. Other programs with minimal fees beyond food and lodging are as follows. For some of these programs you may need to arrange your visa without assistance, maintain your own safety, obtain your own food and lodging, get insurance and understand any legal requirements in a particular area. Thoroughly research any program and area you are considering before you get involved and remain vigilant at all times if you decide to participate:

- Edge of 7—http://www.edgeofseven.org
- WWOOF—http://www.wwoofinternational.org
- Sudan Volunteer Programme—www.svp-uk.com
- United Nations Volunteers—www.unv.org (you must be at least age 25 and already have one degree to participate in this program)
- Volunteer South America—www.volunteersouthamerica.net (this is a listing of many different programs and their web sites with low or no cost volunteer fees in South American countries such as Paraguay, Peru and Ecuador)
- Cloudhead—http://cloudhead.org
- Help Exchange—http://www.helpx.net

Work camps: Work camps are just what they sound like—camps where you work. Groups of people from all over the world are involved in a specific project at each camp. Projects are unique opportunities for individuals to make a significant difference in the countries in which they are situated. For example, projects range from educating youth to environmental conservation to restoration of a medieval castle to the actual building of school in an impoverished country.

Volunteers for Peace coordinates work camps in more than a hundred countries. For more information, contact Volunteers For Peace, Inc., 7 Kilburn Street, Suite 316, Burlington, Vermont 05401, phone: (802) 540-3060, e-mail: info@vfp.org, web site: http://www. vfp.org. You can also explore Community Service Volunteers, 237 Pentonville Road, London, NI 9NJ, England, e-mail: information@ csv.org.uk or volunteer@csv.org.uk, web site: http://www.csv.org.uk

Farming: The WOOF (Working for Organic Growers) Organization was established to give people the opportunity to gain experience in the field of organic farming and gardening in exchange for volunteer work on a farm. For more information on volunteering, visit http://www.wwoofinternational.org.

Field research: With Earthwatch, volunteers work with scientists on field research projects to collect field data in the areas of rainforest ecology, wildlife conservation, marine science, and archaeology. Expeditions are located in areas throughout the world including Africa, Asia, Europe, the Caribbean, and the Middle East. Contact Earthwatch Institute, 114 Western Ave, Boston, MA 02134, phone: (800) 776-0188 or (978) 461-0081, fax: (978) 461-2332, e-mail: info@earthwatch.org, web site: http://www.earthwatch.org.

STUDENT HIGHLIGHT

Volunteering abroad was definitely a revelation for Dave Hicks, a student at Texas A & M University (TAMU). Dave, a mechanical engineering major, volunteered for two summers with a Christian mission agency in Lesotho, an enclave within the Republic of South Africa. Dave talks about his experience: "The summers in Africa changed my life. I am much more globally minded and aware of other cultures. When I returned to school after my volunteer experience abroad, I became very active in the international student community at TAMU, which includes over 4,000 students with a multitude of different cultural backgrounds. My involvement in Lesotho and with the international students at TAMU has been an eye-opening, fun, and interesting experience."

Study Abroad

Studying abroad can add a new dimension to your education. Not only can you improve your foreign language skills, you can experience a new culture and enjoy the international flavor of learning. Being abroad is also a great way to become truly independent. After my best friend left me in Belgium, I was miserable and felt terribly alone. However, after two days of feeling sorry for myself, I began to enjoy my independence and travel solo. By the time I left the country and came home to America, I had a new perspective on my ability to cope independently. Believe me, it gave me a tremendous sense of power.

Evelyn Trujillo, associate professor of foreign languages at Florida Agricultural and Mechanical University, feels that studying abroad is an excellent opportunity for students. Students who study abroad become more aware of global affairs and begin to register individual differences between themselves and the residents of foreign countries. In Professor Trujillo's opinion, students absorb the culture and can thus form their own realistic ideas and opinions of the countries in which they live and study.

You should consider many things when deciding to study abroad. For example, you will need to research the various programs and countries in which they are offered. Look at the subject areas and the course credit and determine whether your own university or college will accept the credit. Other considerations are the duration of the program, the costs, housing arrangements, and the financial aid available. Many study abroad programs can be undertaken for the same amount of tuition you pay—or less—at the school you currently attend. Some scholarships are available, and in many cases you can use your financial aid to pay for courses at a university abroad.

STUDENT HIGHLIGHT

Study abroad for Tavia Evans Gilchrist, a graduate of Northwestern University, was an incredible experience she thinks all students should take advantage of. Tavia explains: "I had some international experience before college, but my summer experience in South Africa, just four years after the official end of apartheid, opened my mind to foreign policy and social issues like never before. I was able to take the trip because I found that my scholarship covered thirteen quarters of aid. So I used the extra quarter during the summer after my sophomore year. I think students should plan to study abroad from the first day they hit campus and work it into their schedule."

Hayley Ford, a student at Marquette University, a private university in Milwaukee, Wisconsin, agrees with Tavia. "I am currently studying abroad in Rome, Italy and it is by far the best decision that I have ever made. Through study abroad, not only are you expanding your knowledge of the world, foreign languages, and different cultures, but you are also learning many things about yourself you may have never known. Being so far from home and not being able to go back, you are forced to adapt to a situation and environment where you may not feel completely comfortable. This uneasiness causes you to make some adaptations until you find yourself actually thinking of the place as home."

A Sampling of Study Abroad Programs

American Institute for Study Abroad (AIFS)
College Division
River Plaza
9 West Broad Street
Stamford, CT 06902-3788
Phone: (800) 727-2437
E-mail: info@aifs.com
Web Site: http://www.aifsabroad.com

College Consortium for International Studies
2000 P Street, NW, Suite 503
Washington, DC 20036
Phone: (800) 453-6956 or (202) 223-0330
E-mail: info@ccisabroad.org
Web Site: http://www.ccisabroad.org

Council on International Educational Exchange (CIEE)
300 Fore Street
Portland, ME 04101
Phone: (800) 40-STUDY or (207) 553-4000
Email: studyinfo@ciee.org
Web Site: http://www.ciee.org

Institute of International Education (IIE)
809 United Nations Plaza
New York, NY 10017-3580
Phone: (212) 883-8200
Web Site: http://www.iie.org

International Student Exchange Programs (ISEP)
1655 N Fort Myer Drive, Suite 400
Arlington, VA, USA 22209
Phone: (703) 504-9960
E-mail: info@isep.org
Web Site: http://www.isep.org

International Studies Abroad
1112 W. Ben White Blvd
Austin, TX 78704
Phone: (800) 580-8826 or (512) 480-8522
E-mail: isa@studiesabroad.com
Web Site: http://www.studiesabroad.com

School for International Training
P. O. Box 676, 1 Kipling Road
Brattleboro, VT 05302-0676
Phone: (800) 257-7751 or (802) 257-7751
E-mail: info@worldlearning.org
Web Site: http://www.worldlearning.org

Immersion Programs and Intensive Language Study

Immersion programs are designed to help students become fluent in a foreign language. In an immersion program, you live in a foreign country while studying its language, culture, and customs. As you live in the country and become immersed in day to day activities, your verbal responses in the language become quicker and more correct. During your stay, you are also exposed to real-life situations requiring you to use your knowledge of the host country's language and culture.

For many students, particularly those majoring in foreign language, a program such as this is very beneficial because it requires constant practice and use of a language. If you have ever studied a foreign language, you know how difficult it is to become fluent without practice beyond the classroom. For more information on immersion programs, contact your foreign languages department or other organizations focusing on international study such as those listed in this chapter.

Intensive language study is similar to an immersion program. With an intensive language study program, you are immersed in the language, culture, and customs of a country, but you may not physically be in the country. If you have a short amount of time and want to be exposed to several levels of a language (from beginning to advanced) quickly, an intensive language study program may be a great option for you.

Immersion Programs

Cuernavaca Language School
Phone: +52 777 274-3548
E-mail: clsmexico@yahoo.com.mx or cls@cls.com.mx
Web Site: http://www.cls.com.mx

Louise Harber/Foreign Language Study Abroad Service
P. O. Box 430903
South Miami, FL 33243
Phone: (786) 216-7302
E-mail: info@flsas.com
Web Site: http://www.flsas.com

Intensive Language Study Programs

Summer Language Institute
P.O. Box 400161
Dell 1, Bonnycastle Drive

Charlottesville, VA 22904-4161
Phone: (434) 243-2241
E-mail: uvasli@virginia.edu
Web Site: http://www.virginia.edu/summer/SLI/

9

Other College Opportunities

Countless opportunities are open to you in college; I have discussed many of them throughout this book. Others, such as exchange programs, conferences, contests, and honors programs, will be discussed in this chapter. Many of the opportunities introduced to you may be unique and may not currently exist on your campus. However, this doesn't mean you can't take advantage of them.

You can still participate, either by working with someone at your college or university to get the program started, or by participating in a program or opportunity offered by another college or university. Find someone at your university who is receptive to your ideas and work with them. In many cases, a program or opportunity may already exist without students being aware of it. Thoroughly review your university or college web site. You may discover many unusual opportunities through web pages dedicated to various programs at your university. Also ask around and be observant—that's how I found out about most of the opportunities and programs I have written about. Of course I couldn't cover everything in one book, and your school may well have unique programs, but I hope you've gotten a taste of what's out there.

University Exchange Programs

Are you tired of your university? Want to try out a new one? Get involved with an exchange program and trade places with another student. University exchange programs allow students of one school to study at another within the United States or abroad. Usually the institutions are similar in their educational styles and traditions. For example, students at Spelman College can study domestically at similar institutions like Mount Holyoke, Dartmouth, and Wellesley. This type of exchange program allows you to explore the curriculum and traditions of another educational institution, take courses your university may not offer, or attend the class of a world famous professor or renowned author who teaches at that school.

UNIVERSITY HIGHLIGHT

Spelman College

Spelman College, a women's college in Atlanta, Georgia, offers its students numerous enhancement programs. Among them are exchange programs with colleges including Wellesley College, Mount Holyoke College, Mills College, and Stanford University. Spelman also maintains the Ethel Waddell Githii Honors Program. During the summer students in this program attend professional conferences all over the country in addition to enjoying the benefits of special classes, seminars, discussion groups, and priority housing.

Spelman students can also take advantage of the Women in Science Engineering (WISE) Program which give students the opportunity to experience research training with professional staff at NASA centers. Students accepted into the WISE program receive a stipend and financial assistance covering 50 percent of their tuition, fees, books and supplies, as well as room and board.

Beloit College

Beloit College in Beloit, Wisconsin, offers its students a summer employment program, school-arranged jobs, and internships. Through its office of international education, study opportunities abroad are plentiful, particularly in countries such as Ecuador, Senegal, Russia, and Turkey.

They also have special programs for students interested in the study of psychology in diverse cultural settings abroad. Participants in this special program are immersed in two distinct societies for two seven week periods. Each society normally has sharply contrasting ethnic, religious, linguistic, and geographical characteristics. In each location, currently Tartu, Estonia, and Fez, Morocco, students study cross-cultural psychology, language, history, arts, and literature in translation. They also conduct an independent research project.

Double Major

Can't make up your mind about the area you want to major in? Declare a major in two subjects. Most universities will allow students to complete the requirements of two majors at the same time. If you are interested in having a diverse skill base, a double major is an excellent opportunity for you. Your majors could be totally dissimilar, such as French and computer science, or complementary, such as French and international relations. It might take you longer to graduate and it will certainly require more effort, but if you think it's for you, go for it!

A Minor

A minor is a program of study in which a student takes a number of courses in a discipline that are not enough to be a major, but are more than other courses. A minor is usually a secondary interest to the major. For example, if a student majors in accounting, she could minor in Spanish–the two don't have to be related. The minor generally shows on your academic transcript.

In many instances, college graduates have entered professions in the area of their minor rather than their major—one student might go on to be a Spanish instructor rather than an accountant. In any case, minors give students the opportunity to explore other areas of interest.

3-2, 3-1, 2-2 Programs

3-2, 3-1, and 2-2 are cooperative academic programs involving two postsecondary institutions. For example, in a 3-2 program, you would study at one institution for three years, then transfer to the second for two years. A 2-2 program involves equal amounts of time at each institution; a 3-1 program involves three years at one institution and one at another. For instance, Loyola University in Chicago, Illinois, has a 3-2 pre-engineering program with Columbia University. Students earn a Bachelor of Science (B.S.) in Physics from Loyola and a B.S. in Engineering from Columbia University after spending three years at Loyola followed by two years at Columbia.

Contests & Competitions

Throughout your college career, you will have many opportunities to participate in contests or competitions. Take advantage of every opportunity, even if it isn't necessarily an area of expertise for you. Entering competitions allows you to get feedback on your efforts, which can help you to improve yourself and discover skills in which you didn't know you were proficient. Whether you win or lose, competitions can also add spice to your résumé or the personal statement on your graduate school application. Your competitive experiences will help to form an image of a highly motivated individual in the minds of prospective employers or admissions officers.

Moreover, your participation in competitions and contests could get exposure for you and some pursuits, particularly those that need funding. Other potential benefits of contests are prize money and free trips such as the one David Buckholtz, a student at Emory University, took when he was selected as a winner of the international essay competition organized by the International Student Committee (ISC) at Harvard University. He describes it: "During the spring I was selected as a finalist in the ISC symposium essay contest, which allowed me to visit St. Gallen, Switzerland, for free…The conference was an amazing experience, especially being there with other scholars, but the highlight of my trip was the chance to take some time before the conference and travel around Europe. It was my first trip out of the eastern time zone, not to mention the United States." Travel opportunities are frequently part of worldwide, national, or sometimes even regional competitions.

Contests abound on college campuses all over the world. You can participate in poetry, oratorical, debating, mock trial team, photography, dance, essay, music, and many other types of competitions. Get involved and compete! Competition stimulates your mind and helps you get into practice for the competitiveness of just being alive.

To find out about competitions which you might like to enter, read your campus newspaper and other magazines for college students, or consult your major department. Your dean's and president's offices may be familiar with other competitions. And don't forget to visit your university or college web site often for announcements about upcoming competitions and contests. If you're interested in writing contests, visit the Poets & Writers web site at http://www.pw.org for more information about awards and contests in this area.

You can also use your skills at blogging or texting to enter competitions that could offer you scholarship funds. For example, WyzAnt's, a tutoring service, currently offers an annual college scholarship essay contest where high school and college students can win up to $10,000 in scholarship money. To enter, you complete an entry form and an essay in 300 words or less describing how you will use your education to make an impact on others. After you complete your essay, then you promote your essay using email and social media by contacting friends and family to get votes for your essay. Finalists will be determined by popular vote. Tutors from WyzAnt will then review finalist essays in the final round to determine the winners for scholarships worth $10,000, $3,000, and $2,000! Visit http://www.wyzant.com (see scholarships).

DoSomething.org is a nonprofit for young people and social change focused on causes such as bullying, homelessness and cancer. They have several scholarship programs available and some of them require texting to win scholarships ranging from $2000 to $5000. Several are open to U.S. and Canadian students 25 and under and do not require a minimum GPA. See http://www.dosomething.org (see scholarships).

Collegescholarships.org also has a blogging scholarship for students who maintain a weblog. They award $1000 annually. See http://www.collegescholarships.org/our-scholarships/blogging.htm.

Scholarship programs such as the above may also be a savvy marketing techniques for the companies to promote themselves or certain causes. For some you may need to share information about yourself, encourage others to visit specific web sites or read about certain issues and potentially have numerous marketing efforts directed your way. Just make sure you don't share personal identifying information such as social security numbers, bank account numbers. And if you're wondering about a giveaway, check it out! Also be aware that many of these programs change frequently. An opportunity based on texting, blogging, or social media could be here today and gone just as quickly tomorrow.

The following are a few examples of contests and competitions college students can enter.

St. Gallen Wings of Excellence Award

Web Site: http://www.stgallen-symposium.org

International competition organized by the International Student Committee at the University of St. Gallen. A limited number of student entries in the competition are selected to attend and participate in the International Management Symposium in St. Gallen, Switzerland. The symposium is attended by international leaders in industry, government, academia, and finance. Participants can share their views on the international theme during workshops, panels, and lectures. The deadline for entries is usually in February. Entries may consist of an essay, a scenario, a project report or proposal, a multimedia presentation, or an entrepreneurial concept.

Who's Who Among Students in American Universities and Colleges

Web Site: http://www.whoswhoamongstudents.com

This competition is a recognition program based on the nomination of your school. Contact your student activities or dean's offices for more information. You may have to complete an application and submit an essay or recommendation before being nominated by your university or college for this award.

Honors Program

Honors programs are designed to provide challenging courses and extracurricular activities for high-achieving students and to encourage academic excellence. Some advantages of membership in the honors program (depending on the college) are:

- Possible acceleration in the completion of your general studies requirements;
- Enrollment in classes of reduced size;

- Opportunities for the development of leadership skills through honors activities;
- Individual honors courses and completion of honors program requirements will be listed on your transcript;
- Participation in state, regional, and national meetings of honors councils;
- Honors seminars and other specialized courses;
- Dedicated dormitories or dormitory areas.

I participated in the University Honors Program at Florida Agricultural and Mechanical University for the duration of my undergraduate career. Our advisor, Dr. Ivy Mitchell, encouraged participation in numerous honors council conferences all over the United States. Under her direction, we organized the first and second annual Bernard D. Hendricks Undergraduate Honors Conferences.

Honors program activities helped me develop my leadership, motivational, and teamwork skills. Not only were we made aware of honors-related activities, but we were encouraged to participate in many national contests and programs. Members were also involved in several community service projects that involved mentoring and tutoring students in high school.

Interdisciplinary Programs

Interdisciplinary programs allow students to study or learn about a variety of subjects through classes, seminars, and workshops. In an interdisciplinary program, you get a broader education because you can fully experience two or more subjects. These programs are designed by university departments to provide a grouping of courses or projects taken from various disciplines and focused around a specific theme. You will also become more well-rounded, with familiarity in several fields of study rather than just one.

UNIVERSITY HIGHLIGHT

Students at Boston College in Chestnut Hill, Massachusetts, have many unique extracurricular experiences to choose from. This college emphasizes interdisciplinary programs in its quest to produce well-rounded students with a holistic view of world. The college offers more than a dozen interdisciplinary programs of study, which include American studies, environmental studies, and international studies.

One service learning program, PULSE, is designed to help students get involved in social and field service work while satisfying their course requirements for philosophy and theology. As a participant in the program a student might serve as a companion to a disabled adult, tutor an inmate, offer a sympathetic ear to a suicidal person during a phone conversation, or feed a homeless person on a cold winter night.

Early Admission Programs

Degree programs at certain professional schools will allow some pre-professional students to enroll immediately after their junior year at an undergraduate school. These are usually programs in business, law, and medical schools and are reserved for students who show exceptional talent and have impressive academic records. With this option you can either shorten the usual time needed to earn both undergraduate and graduate degrees from a professional school, or you can guarantee your eventual admission to the school early and begin preparing for those studies early. At Fordham College at Rose Hill in New York (FCRH), the 3-3 program allows students to enter Fordham University's School of Law after three years of study at FCRH. After completing the first year of law school, students are awarded their Bachelor of Arts or Bachelor of Science degree.

Conferences/Forums

Conferences are formal meetings usually arranged by an association for the benefit of its countrywide member chapters. These meetings involve panel discussions with experts on topics of interest to the members. They may also include self-help workshops on areas such as managing finances, developing good study habits, and managing time wisely. There is always at least one keynote speaker, usually a recognized expert in the field or an author.

The benefits of attending conferences are numerous. As an attendee, you can absorb ideas from other students, converse with experts from diverse fields, develop a network of contacts, listen to inspiring speakers, and take home new information to apply to your life. At many of the conferences I attended, members of the organization were given the opportunity to present and lead sessions in keeping with the theme of that year's conference. This is an excellent way to develop your presentation and public speaking skills. Also, if you're interested in graduate school, these conferences are good ways to expand your ideas and opinions in a particular field, since most of the presentations are based on an individual's own research in an area.

You don't necessarily have to be a member to attend an organization's conference, since many require all attendees to pay a fee to come anyway. As a non-member you can pay a fee as well, although it is usually higher. The conferences you would be interested in attending as a college student might even be paid for by your university, as mine were.

I attended many conferences while at Florida Agricultural and Mechanical University. They were in interesting cities including San Antonio, St. Louis, and Washington, DC. Exploring the city is an added bonus after you've attended several sessions during the day. Tours were usually arranged for those who wanted to explore as a group.

One of the most memorable experiences of my undergraduate years was attending a conference sponsored by the National Collegiate Honors Council. At this conference several notable speakers gave presentations, but in my opinion, the best and most inspirational was the writer Nikki Giovanni. Her excellent speech touched on many of today's important issues. Although speaking on these issues is not unique to her, as many speakers touch upon them at some point for emphasis and impact, the excellence of her talk stemmed from her ability to relate her viewpoint in a humorous yet soulful and touching manner. I wanted to laugh, cry, and scream all at once. Giovanni talked about growing old, race relations, family, love, and a host of other topics. Her comments were extremely well-presented and focused, even though they covered a spectrum of ideas. To this day, she ranks as one of the best speakers I ever heard.

10

Life After Class

In *Top Performance, Zig* Ziglar, a key motivational speaker, mentions a study conducted jointly by the Stanford Research Institute and the Carnegie Foundation. He emphasizes one of the key findings supported by the study: "15 percent of the reason you get a job, keep a job, and move ahead in that job is determined by your technical skills and knowledge … regardless of your profession. The other 85 percent has to do with your people skills and people knowledge." The best way to gain people knowledge is by dealing with others in some extracurricular activity, thus developing your networking, leadership, and interpersonal skills.

Most college students spend approximately fifteen to eighteen hours a week in class. That leaves several hours to get involved in extracurricular and other activities that can help you realize leadership potential you never knew you had. As a participant or a leader in a particular activity, you can develop a sense of teamwork and encounter challenges you might never have found in the classroom.

Whether your time is devoted to a sorority, a community group, a sport, or any other activity, you have a unique opportunity for personal development you can use throughout your life. While you're doing it, you are also developing a diverse base of friends, associates, and contacts with similar interests. Charity Avery, a junior at the University of Tennessee majoring in special education interpreting and psychology agrees, According to Charity, "It is very important to participate in activities . . . because it broadens your network, builds your résumé, and exposes you to diversity."

If someone asked me to tell them the most important thing he should know about a college education, I would tell him that if you are college student and you don't get involved, you haven't really learned a thing. The college education is a full experience. It does not begin with classes and professors and end with a degree and a job. College is a total body experience. You grow in the mind, in the body, and in the spirit. If you don't, then you have missed out.

This development can take place in many ways. If you get involved with extracurricular activities it will continue to pay off long after you've left college. Getting involved not only makes you a more well-rounded individual, it can also help you in finding a job or hobby, getting into graduate school, or even meeting your mate. Where other résumés may have gaping holes, loads of white space, or colorful graphics, your résumé will have parliamentarian, student government, junior class officer, member of the basketball team or choir, or resident assistant to enhance and complete it, thus showing you as a well-rounded and mature individual who can handle a variety of activities and still perform academically. This is what both employers and admissions officers at graduate and professional schools want to see. Even if graduate school or a job is not your primary goal, extracurricular activities can be a lot of fun and give you a sense of wholeness. You have the opportunity to enjoy ideas, experiences, and achievements with students who share your interests.

Amelia Mehtar, a student at Case Western Reserve University comments on her activities: "I think the activities beyond the classroom are where a majority of learning takes place. In extracurricular activities you learn more about who you are, how you function with others, what you love, what you hate, and what makes you tick. These activities help you explore your interests and truly learn some of life's lessons about teamwork and your ability to achieve. Discovering my leadership potential was one of the most eye-opening and exhilarating experiences of my life; and it would not have been possible without my involvement in activities outside the classroom."

Likewise, Roberto Lopez Jr., a law student at Baylor University and University of Tennessee-Austin graduate, also believes activities are especially important. He says, "Being a member of the conflict resolution center as an undergraduate at the University of

Texas in Austin allowed me to be a state certified mediator and granted me the skills to become more effective at handling disputes."

Finding an organization to join, meeting to attend, or an opportunity to take advantage of should be as simple as taking a leisurely stroll around campus. Each year most campuses hold a fair to acquaint students with the various activities available on campus. Your student activities office also has information about groups on campus, as does your student life handbook. You may also be able to find a list of activities on campus bulletin boards or on your school's web site.

I recently walked around three separate college campuses and picked up no less than fifty flyers, postcards, and bulletins. All of them were advertising campus meetings, new student organizations, volunteer activities, church groups, and so on. Your campus newspaper, radio station, and television station are other sources for information about groups and upcoming meetings and events.

Review groups on social media such as Facebook, Twitter and Instagram. Get connected with them in cyberspace, then connect face to face whenever you can. Helping others to associate your face and personality with your user name is one of the best ways to build your network of contacts.

Following are just a few of the organizations you may be able to find and get involved in on your campus or in the community. Your participation in extracurricular activities and your membership in certain groups could also be an opportunity for scholarship consideration. Often associations and some societies will make scholarships available to members. For example, Alpha Chi, a national college honor society, awards twenty-one national scholarships and fellowships to individual members. Alpha Lambda Delta, which is an honor society for freshman, also awards scholarships and fellowships to members. In fact, all but a few of the honor societies listed below have scholarships available to members. Contact the web site or the national headquarters to find out if a group you belong to has an available scholarship or fellowship opportunity.

Organizations and Activities

Note: Go beyond the web sites listed. Find these organizations on social media such as Facebook, Twitter and LinkedIn. Get connected with them to help build your network and become even more involved with their activities.

Scholastic Honor Societies

(Some organizations below can be joined only by invitation)

Alpha Chi (http://www.harding.edu/alphachi)
Alpha Kappa Mu (http://www.alphakappamu.org)
Alpha Lambda Delta (http://www.nationalald.org)
Blue Key (http://www.bluekey.org)
Cardinal Key (http://www.cardinalkey.org)
Circle K (http://www.circlek.org)
Gamma Beta Phi (http://www.gammabetaphi.org)
Golden Key International Honour Society (http://www.goldenkey.org)
Lambda Sigma (http://www.lambdasigma.org)
Phi Beta Kappa (http://www.pbk.org)
Phi Eta Sigma (http://www.phietasigma.org)
Phi Kappa Phi (http://www.phikappaphi.org)
Phi Theta Kappa (http://www.ptk.org)

Honorary Recognition Societies, Fraternities, and Sororities Related to Field of Study

(Some organizations below can be joined only by invitation)

Business, Finance & Economics

Alpha Beta Gamma - Business (http://www.abg.org)
Beta Alpha Psi - Finance (http://www.bap.org)
Beta Gamma Sigma - Business (http://www.betagammasigma.org)
Delta Mu Delta - Business (http://www.deltamudelta.org)
Phi Beta Lambda - Business (http://www.fbla-pbl.org)
Phi Chi - Business and Economics (http://www.phichitheta.org)

Omicron Delta Epsilon - Economics (http://www.omicrondelta
epsilon.org)

Math & Science

Beta Beta Beta - Biology (http://www.tri-beta.org)
Beta Kappa Chi - Science (http://www.betakappachi.org)
Kappa Mu Epsilon - Mathematics (http://www.kappamuepsilon.org)
Phi Lambda Upsilon - Chemistry (http://www.philambdaupsilon
.org)
Pi Mu Epsilon - Mathematics (http://www.pme-math.org)
Pi Kappa Delta - Forensics (http://www.pikappadelta.com)
Sigma Pi Sigma - Physics (http://www.sigmapisigma.org)
Upsilon Pi Epsilon - Computer Science (http://upe.acm.org)

Medicine, Nursing & Pharmacy

Alpha Epsilon Delta - Pre-Medicine (http://www.nationalaed.org)
Alpha Omega Alpha - Medicine (http://www.alphaomegaalpha.org)
Kappa Psi - Pharmaceutical (http://www.kappapsi.org)
Lambda Kappa Sigma - Pharmacy (http://www.lks.org)
Phi Delta Epsilon - Medicine (http://www.phide.org)
Sigma Theta Tau - Nursing (http://www.nursingsociety.org)

Language & Communications

Alpha Epsilon Rho - Broadcasting (http://www.nbs-aerho.org)
Delta Phi Alpha - German (http://www.deltaphialpha.org)
Kappa Tau Alpha - Journalism and Mass Communication (http://
www.kappataualpha.org)
Pi Delta Phi - French (http://www.pideltaphi.org)
Sigma Delta Pi - Spanish (http://www.sigmadeltapi.org)
Sigma Tau Delta - English (http://english.org)

Engineering

Eta Kappa Nu - Electrical and Computer Engineering (http://www.
hkn.org)
Omega Chi Epsilon - Chemical Engineering (http://www.che.uto
ledo.edu/oxe)

Pi Tau Sigma - Mechanical Engineering (http://www.pitausigma.net)
Tau Alpha Pi - Engineering Technology (http://www.taualphapi.org)
Tau Beta Pi - Engineering (http://www.tbp.org)

Music

Mu Phi Epsilon - Music (http://www.muphiepsilon.org)
Pi Kappa Lambda - Music (http://www.pikappalambda.org)
Sigma Alpha Iota - Music (http://www.sai-national.org)
Tau Beta Sigma - Band (http://www.tbsigma.org)

Humanities, Social Science, and Other Fields

Alpha Zeta - Agriculture (http://www.alphazeta.org)
Kappa Delta Pi - Education (http://www.kdp.org)
Phi Alpha - Social Work (http://www.phialpha.org)
Phi Alpha Theta - History (http://www.phialphatheta.org)
Phi Upsilon Omicron - Family and Consumer Science (http://www.phiu.org)
Pi Gamma Mu - Social Sciences (http://www.pigammamu.org)
Pi Sigma Alpha - Political Science (http://www.pisigmaalpha.org)
Psi Chi - Psychology (http://www.psichi.org)
Sigma Xi - Scientific Research (http://www.sigmaxi.org)
Upsilon Pi Epsilon - Computer Science (http://upe.acm.org)

To explore additional honor societies, contact the Association of College Honor Societies at (517) 351-8335 or http://www.achsnatl.org.

Sports and Other Activities

Depending upon your college or university, you may have all of these activities or more. You could also have fewer. If something looks interesting below and it is not available at your campus, ask about it or consider working with your college or university to get the activity started on your campus.

Acting and Theatre Associations	Badminton Club
	Baseball

Curling Team
Cycling Team
Beauty pageants
Bowling
Campus broadcasting
Campus players
Canoeing Team
Cheerleading
Chess
Concert band
Crew
Cross country
College or University Radio
College or University
Television
College or University Web
Site
Dance
Eating club (there really are such
clubs at Princeton University)
Equestrian club
Fencing club
Field hockey
Figure skating club
Flag corps
Football
Fraternities
Frisbee Team or Club
Golf
Gymnastics
Handball
Hunt and Dressage
Ice hockey
Intramurals
Jazz band

Judicial board
Karate
Literary magazine
Majorette
Marching band
Newspaper
Orchestra
Panhellenic council
Pom pom squad
Racquetball
Riflery
Rugby
Running Club
Lacrosse
Sailing Team
Student Athletic Advisory
Committee
Ski Team
Soccer
Social media groups
Softball
Sororities
Student government
Swimming
Tennis
Theatre arts
Volleyball
Water Polo Club
Women's or Men's Rugby
Women's or Men's Water
Polo
Wrestling
Yearbook

STUDENT HIGHLIGHT

Extracurricular activities ruled the life of Jany Allen, a graduate of Georgia Tech. Here's what she had to say about them while she was a student there.

"As far as extracurricular activities go, I spent more time on those than on my schoolwork! I almost dropped out of Georgia Tech (GT) my freshman year to go to Clemson University in Clemson, South Carolina. But I got involved in campus activities at Tech and I'm still here after three years. My freshman year, I headed up a program to increase freshman retention rates by pairing up incoming out-of-state students with current students. Because Tech is so technical, and the students are so focused, it can be unfriendly at times. I don't have a technical bone in my body, so I was forced to find non-science and non-math programs for 'people, people' like myself. Luckily, Tech is great when it comes to the diversity of its student programs. We had over 250 clubs and organizations. I was most involved in the GT alumni association's student programs. I was president of the student alumni association, a group of approximately 200 students that interact with alumni through programs like the mentor program, externship programs, and the ambassadors, a group of student hosts that give tours and keep alumni informed about campus happenings.

"I was also on the Student Foundation's board of trustees. We managed a $350,000 endowment, which funds student groups on campus. The Student Foundation is a philanthropic group that helps to start new clubs and assist current clubs to provide professional development and academic help to their members. My involvement at the alumni association has taught me more than my job or my classes because of the interpersonal relationships I have built. I also know the value of networking, running an effective meeting, motivating volunteers, as well as business and personal etiquette."

Professional Clubs/Societies/Associations

Clubs offer numerous opportunities for you as a college student. Within many departments, students majoring in a particular subject area often form clubs. These clubs serve several functions. For example, within your university's economics club, there may be a department whose members hold regular meetings to discuss issues in the department, form study groups for difficult classes, and discuss job opportunities in their field or in the professions in which they are interested. In addition, the club and its members could have their own study or computer room, as is often the case when a majority of the students in a particular department belong to a club. And they may have accounts for the group to connect and share experiences on social media such as Facebook. The club may also arrange for workshops, seminars, and visitations with professionals to aid the members. In some instances, the club will attend conferences or participate in competitions as a group effort.

Many students who belong to departmental clubs associated with a particular profession such as accounting, economics, engineering, or journalism, will join a corresponding national association such as the National Association of Black Accountants, the American Marketing Association, the National Society of Professional Engineers, or the Society of Professional Journalists. Membership in national organizations can offer numerous extended opportunities.

For example, as a member of a national professional organization, you have access to a diverse network of individuals who can assist you in getting your first job after college, in getting into a prestigious graduate school, in setting up your own business, contributing venture capital for an entrepreneurial venture, or finding you a mentor. Associations exist all over the country, many of them with millions of members. Some of the large national associations maintain job databases for their members. Others hold annual conferences. Many provide e-mail newsletters for their members outlining trends in the associated industry, its outlook, and occasionally listing job opportunities and contacts for members to use in a job search. And many will have a presence on social media platforms such as Facebook, LinkedIn, and Twitter. Stay involved and get connected!

Membership in such an association can also be beneficial if you enter competitions or seek internships, or for those opportunities needing a letter of recommendation, in which case an established association member may be the perfect person to give you one. This would be especially beneficial if you needed the recommendation for something associated with the industry. The member may have special insight to provide you with a recommendation based on the qualities you possess that would be perfect for the opportunity.

Another membership benefit is a chance to get a scholarship or fellowship that the association offers to members. If you are not a member of a professional club, association, or similar organization, you should seriously consider joining one. It could help in your future plans, offering that advantage we all could use. To find associations in your area of study, visit the Internet Public Library at http://www.ipl.org and look for the section titled *Associations on the Net*.

If there isn't a branch of a professional association, club, or honorary society in which you are interested on campus, consider starting one; if the organization allows for campus-based chapters. Contact the national headquarters of the club or society for more details.

The Campus Ministry

The university campus ministry is an organization devoted to the holistic development of you as an individual. It seeks to enrich your spiritual, physical, intellectual, and social well-being through various programs and activities. Within the campus ministry association, there may be several separate organizations committed to different beliefs such as the Jewish students' association, the Bahái campus ministry, the Baptist campus ministry, the Catholic campus ministry, the Latter Day Saints student association, the Muslim campus ministry, or the Orthodox Christian fellowship. College is an exercise in the stimulation of the mind. If you believe in the need for spiritual guidance as well as educational guidance for total contentment in college, joining the campus ministry association is an excellent way to get both.

In addition to special fellowship and worship, your campus ministry may offer all or some of the following opportunities:

Bible study	Emergency funds
Choir	Fellowship dinners
Daily devotional guide	Forums
Dialogues	Leadership development
Discussion groups	Liturgical drama and/or dance

Lock-ins

Newsletter

Orientation magazine

Pastoral counseling

Peace and justice education

Prayer room

Recreation

Retreats

Scholarships and/or loans

Service projects

Social action committees

Social events

Spiritual resource room

Study tours

Support groups

Voter registration

Other Spiritual Organizations

Independent fellowship groups also exist, which may or may not be on your campus. If you are interested in joining, obtaining information, or starting one of these groups on your campus, visit the web sites for more information.

- Fellowship of Christian Athletes–http://www.fca.org
- InterVarsity Christian Fellowship/USA (IVCF)– http://inter varsity.org/

11

Getting Along with Roommates

One of the biggest challenges many students face is getting along with other people, particularly roommates. Whether you stay in a dormitory room on campus or stay off-campus in an apartment, you should remember the following to help you start and stay on good terms with a roommate.

- Open the lines of communication–Greet your roommate and start talking in a friendly manner. Ask some of the following questions:
  - Where are you from?
  - Why did you decide to come to this university? What do you like about it?
  - What are you planning to major in?
  - Do you play any games (for example, board games, cards, video games, fantasy football)?
  - If they have a smart phone or tablet, start a game app with them such as the popular, "Words with Friends." If you're really good, make sure you remember some individuals can't handle losing, so try not to beat them constantly or at least too easily. It might destroy your budding relationship. On the other hand, some people thrive on competition and it could make your relationship stronger.
  - Find them on Facebook, Twitter or other social media. This gives you an opportunity to learn something about them to form a basis for starting a conversation.
- Establish common ground–Once you start talking and asking questions, focus on areas you have in common, such as background, home state or city, a love of reading,

or rock climbing. This will help give you a jump-start for lively discussions on topics you both really enjoy and can hopefully help you become friends or at least happy acquaintances with your roommate. Stephen Schorn, a student at the University of Virginia suggests: "Go out with your roommate. Even if you don't like parties, go out somewhere on the grounds. The first few days before school starts there are tons of events going on–going with someone as new to the school as you are means you are in the same boat, plus you get to know them better when you see what they may or may not enjoy doing."

- Discuss boundaries–If you own certain items that are off-limits, let your roommate know. However do it in a friendly manner and be prepared for them to let you know about items that are off-limits to you too. You should have the "keep away," discussion in a friendly non-combative manner. For example, if you don't want someone to use your laptop, say something like, "I have a laptop but I really can't let anyone use it. It's my life and it would cost more than I have to replace it or its contents." Or in the case of food, "I love blackberries. Anything else in the refrigerator, I'm happy to share but please, please let me hoard those for myself."

- It's not forever–If you and your roommate just can't seem to understand or like each other, focus on remembering your relationship is only temporary. There's always next semester or quarter. Or you can visit your resident advisor, dorm counselor, university ombudsman, or housing office to discuss a switch if it becomes too unbearable.

- If possible, avoid lending or borrowing items–Even if you and your roommate have become friends, this practice may not be a good idea. In the words of Shakespeare, "Neither a borrower nor a lender be; for loan oft loses both itself and friend." This means borrowing or lending can lead to the early end of your roommate relationship. If you do lend, always be prepared for the non-return of your items or money. So don't lend anything you can't replace.

- Make it legal–One of the best ways to solve verbal disputes is to have written and signed agreements. If you and your roommate enter into a verbal agreement about items such as an apartment rental or loan, put your agreement in writing. Then, you and your roommate should both sign the agreement. Visit one of the campus law professors to get additional information about resources for putting together a legally binding written contract. Many campuses have at least one lawyer teaching classes or conducting seminars. Or you can visit http://www.nolo.com for online law resources.

12

Romantic Relationships

Hayley Ford, an accounting and international business major at Marquette University, advises students. "Don't rush into a relationship early on. I saw a lot of girls and guys who paired off right away and didn't get to experience college as much as everyone else. Although the excitement of being away from your family and surrounded by so many people your age may be tempting, wait a little while before committing yourself to someone." She also comments, "I have grown more through what I have learned from different activities I've participated in and from the people I have encountered while doing them, than I have learned in the classroom by far."

Based on Hayley's experience romantic relationships that become very intense and monopolize your time can certainly limit your activities. On the other hand, some students such as Richard Rusczyk and Dave Hicks, have found their life mate on a college campus. In an e-mail, Richard, a graduate of Princeton University writes: "I met my wife in my eating club . . . a very high proportion of the interesting conversations I had in college were just before or after meals at the club." Also, when asked to describe the most fun experience he had while in college, Richard wrote, "Probably when my wife said, 'Yes.'"

Similarly, Dave, a graduate of Texas A & M University says his most fun experience was "when I met my wife, whom I married one week after graduation!"

What does this mean to you? It means it's okay to have a romantic relationship. However it is not all right to let the relationship sidetrack you from your goals. This would include an unplanned pregnancy, barely passing or not passing classes due to excess time spent with your love interest, and focusing on your college love to the exclusion of all else. If you've read the chapter, "On Track to Graduate–Time Management and Staying on Schedule," and determined your personal path to graduation, stick with it. If you find love along the way, take your partner along for the ride. Just don't miss out on opportunities as you both explore life together on campus and beyond.

A Few Do's and Don'ts for College Romance

- Do realize you may not find a life partner in college. That's okay.

- Do consider group dates with friends you can trust, especially when you are just starting to get to know someone.

- Do use social media to learn a little more about your potential boyfriend or girlfriend. If you're friends with them on Facebook, do they share every detail about their lives? If yes, then those details could include you if you get involved with them. Do they post or tweet items, comments, or photos you strongly disagree with? If so, consider a relationship with them very carefully. Differences of opinion between you and your significant other are okay. But you don't want to have drastically different values and opinions. It could cause constant tension in your relationship.

- Do take advantage of all opportunities even if they will take you away from your boyfriend or girlfriend. When I was in college, my boyfriend of two years expressed serious dismay about my decision to intern in Brussels, Belgium for the summer. However it never crossed my mind to forgo the internship. I went and it was one of the best decisions I've ever made.

- Do cultivate your friendships beyond your significant other. Your romantic relationship may or may not last but your friendships could last a lifetime.

- Do take your time. You don't have to find someone immediately.
- Do not try to synchronize your class schedule with that of your romantic interest.
- Do not use social media such as Facebook, Twitter or Instagram to air your relationship issues, good or bad.
- Do realize your romantic life on a college campus is very different from how your romantic life could be after college. Take time to evaluate your relationship seriously before getting engaged at college or immediately after college. If possible, take some time after you graduate and you both are hopefully in the same city to determine if you are really compatible.
- Do handle a breakup gracefully. If you're both still on campus, treat each other with civility. I know it will be hard. But it will not help if you foster a negative atmosphere around you. It also will not help if you air your breakup and any problems on social media. Before you vent your anger, take a few moments to breathe and think about the consequences of any action you take. Then ask yourself these questions:
  - Will expressing my anger and frustration really make a difference?
  - Could any of my actions or words while expressing my anger come back to haunt me?
  - Is this person really worth it?
    - For this question, I used to start a list (I never included their name) of all things that really irritated me about a person or our relationship. I made sure the list was a living document I consistently added on to. It would usually become so long I never got to any positive points.

- Do ask the tough questions about issues that matter to you. For example, do you know their goals? Where do they want to live? What do they see themselves doing in 5 years, 10 years, or more? Do they believe in marriage? Are they solely focused on climbing the corporate ladder or reaching a certain point in their chosen field? Are they more interested in love and family? Do they want to commit a certain portion of their life after college graduation to volunteering (perhaps even abroad)? Most importantly, do their answers coincide with your life goals?

- Do realize you may never another opportunity to meet as many potential life partners who hopefully have the same goals as you do.

- Don't lose sight of your educational goals. Once attained, your college degree can be an asset you never lose. Unfortunately a relationship may not last. If you allow a relationship to distract you from the goal of attaining your degree, it can be very hard to finish a degree years later. Just ask anyone who decided to stop college to get married and then 5, 10, 15 or 20 years later still haven't finished but desperately want to do so.

- Don't forget your reputation. When you begin your college career, you have a chance to make impressions and build relationships with many new people. If you choose to do so, your freshman year can be a time to reinvent yourself. Yes, there may be friends from home but there may be many more who have yet to get to know your new persona.

- Don't base a relationship solely on fun and partying. If you and your love interest don't do anything else with each other, then you may not have a solid basis for a lasting relationship.

- Do not feel pressured to do something you do not want to do. He or she may be cute but could be unsafe for you. Date rape, murder, and assaults *can* happen on a college campus and in a college town. Remember your ABC's — always be careful.

- Do not send pictures, text messages or posts that could be a source of embarrassment later.
- Do not let your romantic interest dominate your life. For example, perhaps they never leave your room or apartment. This could be challenging and a source of discontent if you have one or more roommates. Or, if you're hanging out with friends, your boyfriend or girlfriend should not always be with you, unless you share the same friends with him or her. You should always have some "me" time to develop and grow as an individual.

13

Fun Within The Walls

An important factor in your happiness in college is the amount of entertainment and fun you seek. Some of you may be saying, to your parents' approving nods, "If I party too hard, I might flunk out." That is true, but if you don't have any fun at all, you may bore yourself into depression. As they say, "all work and no play …" The trick to having an excellent academic record along with loads of fun is to achieve a balance between education and entertainment. Although it may be a tenuous balance, it is possible.

My personal philosophy while at college was to work hard and play hard. To do this, I dedicated the majority of my weekdays to getting an education in the classroom and my weekends to getting a life. If you're wondering what fun and entertainment have to do with getting the most out of college education or college survival skills, let me clarify one major point: entertainment and fun are not synonymous with partying and alcohol. Entertainment is any activity that allows the body and mind to relax and you to enjoy being alive and well in the world. It could include a walk in the park, attending a music recital, theater performance, or football game, listening to a speech by a political activist or famous actor, or just having an informal get-together among friends.

The benefits of entertainment are many. First and most important, it is your chance to relax. Second, wherever there are people, you automatically have a valuable playing field to develop possible contacts. You can find out about job opportunities, or even meet a future partner for a business venture at an informal gathering or other social event. You can trade ideas, thoughts, opinions, and dreams. Finally, you could meet the person with whom you would like to share your life.

Special Interest Clubs

Special interest clubs are formed based on the common interests or background of the members. Some of the clubs are associated with a specific city or metropolitan area. For instance, some schools have a DC Metro Club, an Ohio club, an Atlanta Club, and so on. Such clubs usually organize parties, car washes, study sessions, trips home, and newsletters. At the very least these clubs can provide excellent networking opportunities for you. Other members can put you in touch with the best professors and in general help orient you to life on the college campus.

Other special interest clubs are formed on the basis of cultural heritage or country of origin like the Haitian, Jewish, African, or Caribbean clubs. In these organizations the individual has many opportunities to delve deeper into his or her heritage or background. The clubs also offer networking opportunities, as well as theme parties, group study sessions, organized trips to associated countries, and lots of fun with people who share a common background.

The Greek Life

Greek societies are national corporations with local chapters set up under the direction of the college or university where they are located. Joining a Greek organization can give you a very active social life filled with parties, community activities, and many other programs sponsored by the organization. At many colleges and universities, there are sorority and fraternity houses in which you can live. In these houses you will find a challenging and usually exciting atmosphere and–at times–household chores. This type of communal living sometimes results in significantly lower housing costs as compared to dorm or apartment living.

Joining a fraternity or sorority has several advantages. When you join you often have immediate and continuous opportunities for social interaction. Most sororities and fraternities have a continuous calendar of events and parties scheduled for the entire year and are constantly thinking up new ones. Many of the community events the sorority or fraternity participates in will make a helpful addition to your résumé. A sorority or fraternity is also an excellent way to develop an extensive network of contacts made up of members past and present, which can help you in many endeavors ranging from finding a job to getting a recommendation for graduate school to getting advice or funds for a big project you are undertaking.

As a member, you may also have access to old class handouts on courses, tests, study notes, syllabi, and reference material. Scholarships are sometimes available to you as a member of the fraternity or sorority. And once you become a member, you gain a group of associates with many smaller common interests and a big one—the fraternity or sorority. For Julia Rose Judge, a student at Case Western Reserve University, being in a sorority is wonderful. She says: "I really enjoy sitting around the dining room table in my sorority house and talking with twenty sisters over a meal. I love having such interesting friends who bring their knowledge, opinions, and senses of humor to the table. It is great to have friends that I respect and admire."

College Parties and Pastimes

You will find many entertaining pastimes while at college. For example, there are often fraternity and sorority parties you can attend. At Florida Agricultural and Mechanical University, there were before-Thanksgiving parties, before-Christmas parties, before-the-finals parties, after-the-finals parties, Spring Break jams, and many other excuses to relax. If you aren't a member of a fraternity or sorority you are still welcome to attend—many such parties are open to the general public, although both fraternities and sororities may charge an entrance fee. Many Greek organizations use the parties to raise funds for charitable activities.

For the sports fiend, you can watch many events while at college. These events are sometimes free to students, depending on the school you attend. I loved going to football games. Only *I* never watched the games, I was too busy watching our band, the Marching 100. You will find a variety of sporting events at any college—

basketball games, swimming events, baseball games, wrestling matches, and many other athletic competitions, depending on what your school offers.

If you like to eat and watch movies, and live in a dormitory, pizza parties and dorm movie nights will be fun activities for you. Several residents can share the expense of renting movies and buying pizzas or, as was the case in my dormitory on several occasions, the pizza and the movies were generously provided by the resident assistant or university.

Ashley Chang, a sophomore at the University of Southern California certainly enjoyed her dorm experience. When asked to describe the most fun experience she's had while in college, Ashley exclaims, "Going backstage at the Golden Globe Awards as part of an internship was definitely a memorable experience, but I also loved spending quality time with my close friends at four in the morning in our dorm. We would talk about anything and everything, and occasionally tried to tap dance or exercise—while trying to muffle our voices and laughter (after all, it was 4:00 a.m.). Sounds silly, but I don't think you can do this anywhere but at college—the dorms provide the perfect recipe for great friendships and amazing bonding time, at any time of day or night!"

Recreation in the form of exercise is easy to accomplish at college. Most campuses encompass areas of land, so walking is one way to exercise and relax. Most campuses also have gyms and fitness centers, so you can work out there. You may also be able to join an aerobics or other type of fitness class. You might want to learn karate or tae kwon do, if your university offers them.

The student union is another entertainment option. You can play video games in the game room, surf the Internet, talk with friends in the lounge, or, if your union has one, go to the campus club or eatery for an appetizer and a drink to unwind.

If you're interested in more cultural entertainment, you could attend a play performed by the theater group, watch a dance recital, or listen to a poetry reading. Musical performances by your institution's jazz ensemble group or gospel choir are another option.

Concerts, step shows, and other major events will often be sponsored by the activities office of the student government association. Opportunities for entertainment are abundant on most college campuses. There's always something to do and someone to do it with. It really depends on what you enjoy doing.

14

Working Around Campus

College campuses offer many jobs. Some can be long-term, like working as a librarian's assistant throughout an entire college career, or they can be short-term, like being a testing assistant for a required campus wide test for one day. Campus jobs can be just as exciting and beneficial as an internship. With them, you can acquire networking and interpersonal skills and develop contacts. In addition, having relevant work experience is often the difference between successful and unsuccessful job applicants and can likewise be a key factor in your admission to a graduate or professional school.

A job on your college campus not only provides experience for you, it can expose you to some very important opportunities and people. A job on campus literally could change the direction of your life. Picture this: You work in your dean's office as a staff assistant. The CEO and the president of a major corporation has accepted an invitation to speak at your school. When he arrives in the office, you greet him and chat with him for a couple of minutes before he joins the dean for breakfast. Just before leaving the office, he offers you an internship with his company for the summer because he was so impressed with your insightful conversation. Think this is impossible? Think again.

Not only is it possible, it happened several times to students during my undergraduate years at Florida Agricultural and Mechanical University. At the School of Business and Industry, presidents and CEOs of Fortune 500 companies visited the school on a weekly basis. They and the recruiters who often accompanied them gave speeches and held receptions, and frequently offered internships and co-op opportunities to interested and interesting students.

Gaining valuable work experience is one advantage of getting a job in college, but there are many others: getting references for your future career, adding attractive features to your résumé, acquiring a mentor, and acquiring technical and leadership skills. Depending on the organization, for some jobs you may be able to get credit towards your college degree. In fact, some jobs are created specifically for that reason. That is called cooperative education, and it was discussed in the chapter, "Getting Internships, Cooperative Education and Other Learning Experiences Beyond the Classroom."

Work Study & On Campus Jobs

Work study is another kind of job. The work study program is jointly sponsored by the federal government and your college to offer part-time employment—the government subsidizes the wages paid by the college. Work study is available on most college campuses primarily for students as part of their financial aid packages. Work study jobs can be anywhere on a college campus, including the bookstore, a lab, or the public relations office. With planning, you can obtain work study in an office where you will be able to gain valuable contacts and experience that could help you when participating in contests or applying to graduate school.

For example, a student who aspires to be a photojournalist can work on the campus newspaper. While there, she will get experience, résumé credits, and a portfolio of pictures and articles, and be able to participate in journalism contests. In addition, the advisor for the newspaper can help by critiquing her work and sharing real world experiences with her.

If you are not initially offered work study as part of a financial aid package from your college or university, make sure to inquire later once you join the campus. Since all offers of work study are not accepted by eligible students in their financial aid package, there may be opportunities for you once the school semester or quarter begins. Visit the financial aid office to speak with the individual responsible for work study assignments. Ask to be notified of any work study openings as they become available or ask when you should contact them to inquire about openings. Even if a work study opening doesn't become available, there may be other on-campus job opportunities for you. On-campus jobs are very similar to work study.

Community Service and Volunteering

Community service is important for college students not only for the experience and the opportunity to help the community, but also because it may result in financial aid such as scholarships and awards or college credit. Community service can also add new depth to a résumé or a personal statement for graduate school. In addition, many friends and associates as well as valuable business or social contacts can be made at events benefiting individuals within a community.

Campus Compact, a coalition of more than 1200 colleges and universities, is an organization that aids students in their community efforts. Over the past twenty years, this organization has mobilized millions of students in service to their communities and has also administered funds in the form of service scholarships to students. For more information about this coalition, contact Campus Compact, 45 Temple Place, Boston, MA 02111, phone: (617) 357-1881, web site: http://www.compact.org.

You can also visit web sites such as http://www.volunteennation.org to find volunteer opportunities for a variety of different organizations and communities. Some of these organizations are listed in the following section.

Other Volunteer Organizations

Habitat for Humanity International
Collegiate Challenge
121 Habitat Street
Americus, GA 31709-3498
Phone: (800) HABITAT, ext. 2215
E-mail: colchal@habitat.org
Web Site: http://www.habitat.org

Points of Light
600 Means Street, Suite 210
Atlanta, GA 30318
Phone: (404) 979-2900 or 1-800-Volunteer
Web Site: http://www.pointsoflight.org

Volunteers of America
1660 Duke Street
Alexandria, VA 22314
Phone: (800) 899-0089 or (703) 341-5000
Web Site: http://www.voa.org

STUDENT HIGHLIGHT

As a student at Stanford University, AJ Robinson was seriously involved in his community. In fact, he started getting involved in volunteer work as soon as he began his college career at Stanford and continued his good works even as a graduate student at Harvard University studying political science.

When asked about his charitable activities at Stanford, AJ stated, "I was the co-founder and co-director of a student-run, nonprofit organization designed to empower economically disadvantaged youth from the San Francisco Bay Area. The program was entitled SOAR (Students Offering Alternative Realities) and the kids we worked with ranged in age from fourteen to eighteen. We provided academic tutoring, job training, professional counseling, peer mentoring, and summer jobs. We also conducted an SAT prep class and a host of other weekend workshops. The organization had a staff of approximately twenty-five to forty, depending on the mood and commitment level of the students at Stanford. Community service has changed my life by teaching me the politics behind poverty. It also taught me how to motivate and mobilize a large and diverse population."

Professional Trade Experience & Campus Organizations

Your trade is your eventual occupation. Professional trade experience can be gained by joining any of the numerous campus organizations that practice your trade or your profession as part of the activities associated with your campus. For example, most university campuses have a yearbook, newspaper, radio station, television station, student government, and literary magazine. As a staff member for one of these organizations you can enjoy many benefits, not the least of which is getting work experience to use when you actually enter the job market.

Becoming a part of these organizations could easily get you a job, internship, or a co-op in the appropriate industry. You can also gain valuable contacts through your advisor, who may have already worked as a professional in the television, radio, magazine, or newspaper industry. Likewise, if you are interested in diplomacy and politics, student government offers opportunities. The advisor for student government may also have once been professionally ensconced in politics on a local, state, or federal government level. The individuals you meet while a part of these campus organizations may be able to offer numerous contacts, referrals, and information for furthering your own career. They can serve as excellent sources for advice, mentoring, and recommendations.

You can also participate in contests, attend conferences, forums, and other meetings or retreats associated with your trade. Retreats are usually held for the members of an organization in a popular and occasionally exotic location. During a retreat, meetings and discussions are held on topics of concern to the group members and the university. Organizations may also host a career fair specifically for interested students in their group.

To get the most out of a job in one of these areas, you could try tying your work study to one of these organizations. Doing this means that you could be paid to do something you really enjoy and you think of as your future career!

Some of the staff positions in these campus organizations offer small salaries. While often enjoying relaxing fringe benefits like retreats, student government officials such as president and vice president often get paid a stipend of as much as $10,000 a year or more.

STUDENT HIGHLIGHT

As a political education and history major at the University of California at Los Angeles (UCLA), Rondre Jackson often related his personal experience to his campus job. "I was a well-rounded student who didn't just study. I socialized, got involved in many activities, and worked, all of which really enhanced my college experience. There were many activities in particular that made college rather fun for me. The main ones were: working for the basketball gym (Pauley Pavilion) and being the manager of UCLA's women's basketball team. I firmly believe students should have some work experience while going to school because college is usually the last step before entering the real world of work. A job in college can help you gain experience to prepare for entering this reality.

"I chose to work at Pauley Pavilion because of a deep interest in sports, especially basketball. As an employee, my job mainly offered behind-the-scenes work. However it had huge advantages. I watched and attended all of UCLA's games and sports-related events for free. To me this was the best part, particularly when the men's basketball team went to and won the Final Four. The excitement and adrenaline at that event and just about all the games was exhilarating.

"Earlier during my college career, while I was working for Pauley Pavilion, I was able to get acquainted with the coaches for the women's basketball team. Later I interviewed for the position of manager with the women's basketball team and got it. Being employed as the first male manager of UCLA's women's basketball team began to make my college experience even more unique and quite interesting. As the manager of the team, I began to travel extensively to places like Alaska, Texas, Oregon, Massachusetts, and many other states to which I had never been.

"Even though traveling with the team and visiting all these places and more was a big plus for my job, the friendships made with the players and coaches of the team were even more special than the excitement of traveling. As a manager almost completely surrounded by women, I began to gain a new perspective on the way females should be treated. I now feel like I have an extended family of sisters I'll remember forever.

"Not only did I become a well-seasoned traveler, and a male sensitive to the needs of women, I also picked up a lot of organizational skills that I feel really help in the real world. Managing a team includes many organizational and scheduling activities such as handling and ordering uniforms, arranging study hall, and preparing for meals. My job on campus opened up a whole new world for me and I loved it!"

Rondre offers his personal tips for college survival and enhancement:

- "Don't wait until the last minute. A lot of surviving in college is based on organizational-related activities. Time management for every type of situation is a must. If I hadn't been a good manager of my time, there is no way I could have done so much as the manager of the women's basketball team."

- "Do take advantage of the services and activities provided while in college, such as career placement and counseling. College tuition can be very expensive yet all kinds of services are provided. If you use them, it will definitely help you feel you have gotten the most out of your college experience and the most for your buck."

- "After graduating, think about the things you got the most out of in college and use those skills as decision makers to make choices for life after college. For example, I really enjoyed being a manager for the basketball team. Although I still had a strong interest in attending law school after I graduated, I considered and eventually made the decision to become a coach for a few years, either at UCLA or another college or university. I certainly had the contacts and developed the skills for it. Whatever path my career takes, I still have my degree, many friends and contacts, many special memories, and the experience of managing a team for a major university."

15

Networking and Professional Development

Networking is the process of taking advantage of all opportunities that cross your path to develop professional contacts and explore or uncover new job opportunities that could result in knowledge of job leads, important business information, or trends in the world. At various points throughout your life you will have to do some networking, whether to find a job, keep a job, or further your own business. Networking can take place just about anywhere and with almost anyone. Although there are some common established places to network, such as career fairs, receptions, social media and so on, you can network just as easily at a friend's home, at the local gym, or in your favorite professor's office. Anytime you speak with others who have information that helps you uncover a job lead or a contact, you are networking.

Marquette University student, Hayley Ford, agrees. According to Hayley, "Whether it is a classmate, professor, or organization advisor, college is the time to meet so many different people and also make contacts that may become very beneficial to you in the long run."

Networking can help you in many ways. In addition to helping with job leads, networking can boost your confidence level and help you acquire mentors. It gives you an opportunity to exchange and receive information from individuals at many levels. As you build on your network, you can continually get advice from those you have added to the chain. You must remember, however, that networking is a two-way process, much like communication— there is a giver and a receiver, and the roles are always changing.

When others assist you, they may expect something in return. If a recruiter tells you about a job opening in his company, he will expect you to be an exemplary employee for his company or certainly an interviewee who reflects well on him. If you find a mentor, she may expect you in turn to mentor someone else she recommends, or at the very least to reflect well on her by applying the knowledge or advice she has given you. If a friend gives you a job lead or contact name, sometime in the future he may expect you to return the favor.

Networking is one of the very best ways to get an internship, job offer, or other exciting opportunity. Many think uploading a résumé to every online database they can find is the ultimate way to find a job, internship or research opportunity. It's not. Ask around. Through networking, you'll find many professionals and other students who have discovered and secured some amazing opportunities via individuals they knew and stayed in contact with, not through an online job search. For those of you who believe in all things technological, you can power charge your networking with social media platforms such as LinkedIn and Facebook. Staying in touch with those you know and keeping them abreast of your skills, both new and old, will open the doors of opportunity for you now and in the future!

Receptions

A great way to network is by attending receptions held by corporations and organizations visiting your school. Most receptions are held the night before a day of on-campus interviewing. Getting to know your interviewer beforehand is always an advantage for you— you will be more relaxed at the interview and the atmosphere will likely have warmed from inquisitive stranger to friendly acquaintance. Also, you will be armed with more information and insight about the company and its opportunities, which can help you relate for the interviewer how your skills and experience match the company's needs. You can also visit a company's Facebook, Twitter or other social media platform to gain some insight about the company, its values, the mission, and its goals. If the company is tweeting or posting about something, the topic or event may be of great concern to them. Or your knowledge of their tweets and posts could be your key to understanding their latest marketing campaign or corporate focus. At the very least your social media research will give you something to discuss with the company representative.

Receptions usually last from one to three hours. They often consist of a general introduction to the company by its representatives (recruiters from the company), brochures, applications and tables of finger food. For approximately one hour, representatives will regale you with the merits of the company through a spectacular PowerPoint presentation or video or testimonials from past interns and current employees of the company. The rest of the time is spent mingling with the representatives and others like you, asking pertinent questions about the company, its future, and the opportunities it has to offer. If you can speak to a representative one-on-one, it can be an important opening for you not only to have some of your questions answered, but to briefly describe yourself, talk a little about your background, and help him or her understand what you have to offer the company if they hire you as an intern, co-op, or permanent hire.

Remember, however, that this is not an interview; give others a chance to speak, too. If you're familiar with the phrase "work the room," it definitely applies here as you repeat this question and answer exchange with as many of the company representatives as possible (for varied perspectives) before the night is over.

For more information on receptions, as well as a list of receptions being held at your school or at a local hotel for students from your school, contact your career center. They'll be more than happy to help.

College Recruitment Conferences/Job Fairs

Another excellent way to develop contacts or further a job search is to attend college recruitment conferences. Conferences and job fairs may be held locally at a convention center or other major venue, or at another location in the nearest major city. They are attended by hundreds of recruiting officials from numerous companies. Students are expected to dress in business attire and have copies of their résumé ready to distribute. Some companies may also interview you immediately after talking with you briefly during the conference or job fair.

I first learned about conferences and other opportunities, including receptions, interviews, and information sessions, by reading our campus newspaper. Many companies will announce events they are sponsoring in your school newspaper, radio station, TV station, web site, Facebook page or other social media platform. Paying attention to campus media is important not only to keep abreast of campus events, but also to discover networking opportunities. You should also contact your career development center and get connected with them online. And make sure to check out your local media as well. You may even want to conduct an advanced Internet search as explained in chapter 7 to find local job fairs and conferences.

Career Fairs

Career fairs are similar to college recruitment conferences. They are generally sponsored by the individual college's career center, and are attended by recruiters from companies in various fields. Because these events are on a smaller scale (the size of your student body) there is not the clamoring for the recruiters' attention you might find at the region-wide conferences. Therefore speaking with a representative and handing her your résumé while explaining its finer points should be a little easier (unless, perhaps you attend a huge university).

Even if you are not in search of a job, career fairs are great for networking and learning more about companies in which you may later be interested. Bing Spitler, former manager of college and university relations at Armstrong World Industries, says he wishes more students would attend career fairs earlier in their undergraduate career. He feels if they did, it would give them more time to get to know the company and for the company to get to know them and see their development over the years. Also note your early attendance at a career fair could give you an opportunity to connect with a valuable contact through your LinkedIn page. This might come in handy later.

Associations

Since many of the members in an association have numerous contacts in a particular field, becoming a member of or contacting associations in your field are also ways to network. Association members know who to call and often are in positions themselves to help you obtain a permanent job offer, get into graduate school, or win a prestigious fellowship. Contacting these organizations could result in your eventual membership if you're not a member already. Some benefits of membership you may want to consider are job leads, access to member magazines and articles to help you find a job or get into graduate school, information on current salaries in the field, and if you're in need of funds to finish your college education, they may have member scholarships too.

Many associations also hold annual conferences, which you could attend as either a member or a non-member. If you're interested in learning which associations are related to your field of study, refer to the *Encyclopedia of Associations*, published by Gale Research. This encyclopedia can usually be found in your local library. To find other associations in your area of interest, visit the Internet Public Library at http://www.ipl.org and refer to the section, *Associations on the Net*. This section is organized by category. So if you're looking for associations affiliated with law, you can go directly to the web page.

Interviews

Although you may think a job interview can have only one purpose, interviews are often an excellent source for contacts. You might interview with a company for one position but then be considered for an entirely different job within the same company or in another division or subsidiary. This happened to me twice when I was interviewing.

I interviewed with a major banking corporation for a permanent job position. During the interview, the recruiter called in another recruiter from the company to talk to me. Months later, the second recruiter called to see if I would be interested in a position at another bank—he had left the original company but remembered our interview. Not only that, my résumé had been put in an online job bank by someone else and the recruiter had recognized the distinctive border and type style I used as he was looking in the job bank for prospective candidates.

In another situation, I had a second interview, or plant visit, with a company at the corporate headquarters. As is usually the case in second interviews, I met with several individuals separately. During one interview session, I was asked if I would be interested in a position in their accounting department, even though I was there as a candidate for their sales division. Although I did not choose to work for the company, I gained a unique contact during this interview. This contact would have been very helpful, had I decided to work for the company, and may still be helpful if I decided to seek a position outside of my current employer.

What does this mean? It means that in every meeting you can—and should—make a lasting impression and a valuable contact. Personal contacts are invaluable when it's you and many others being considered for one position. Not only was this interview a networking situation, my résumé was also a networking tool.

Information Sessions

Information sessions are given by companies to allow students to become familiar with both the overall organization and the opportunities available. During an information session, a corporate recruiter will usually give a brief presentation or show a video. Then they will answer questions. Alumni from your school who are currently employed are often present to give a brief summation of their own experiences and responsibilities with the company. Such sessions are a great opportunity for you to establish a basic contact with a company or organization in which you're interested. Be sure to bring your business card (see the *Networking Tools* section later in this chapter) and at least five current copies of your résumé. Hand out your business cards generously. Hoard your résumé unless you are specifically asked for a copy.

Faculty and Staff

The faculty and staff at your university are good contacts to have in your networking database. Many of them have important and sometimes powerful contacts in the world beyond your campus. They can be an excellent source for job leads, insider information, advice, referrals, or to serve as a mentor. Developing relationships with faculty and staff members is one of the first steps to creating an effective network for your on- and off-campus activities, as well as other future endeavors. You can also connect with them on social media platforms such as LinkedIn and Facebook.

Graduate and Professional School Days

Graduate and professional school days combine the characteristics of career fairs *and* college fairs you may have attended during high school when you were deciding on which college to attend. At graduate and professional school days, as at career fairs, you are seeking information to help further your future. Moreover, during graduate and professional school days, as at college fairs, you are still focusing on your future, but with a professional educational focus. More specifically, graduate and professional school days are usually sponsored by the university to provide information about specific graduate and professional programs and fellowships.

Hundreds of recruiters set up booths to provide you with information about the school, the success rates of their programs, the fellowships available, and to answer your questions. Such an event allows you the perfect opportunity to develop contacts and relationships with admissions officials and student representatives who could help you gain acceptance to the program or lead to a mentoring relationship or a prestigious fellowship award.

Networking Tools

For effective networking you need to have certain tools. Your experiences, your personality, and the impression you make are tools that will naturally follow you everywhere you go. Other tools you will need for the networking include business cards, a résumé, a cover letter, an introductory letter, a follow-up letter, and online address books and contact lists. You should also have a LinkedIn page. When coupled with your natural networking tools, these will make a lasting impression and can help a contact conjure up a visual picture of you.

Business Cards

You should seriously consider having business cards made. Business cards are fairly inexpensive, costing around $20 to $30 for a thousand. If you have decent computer skills and have mastered a word processing software program such as Microsoft Word, you can create your own in minutes. You can then print camera-ready copy on a laser printer (if you don't have a computer or printer, use those available elsewhere on campus). After you have printed it, copy stores like Office Depot will print your cards using the camera-ready copy or electronic file with which you have supplied them. The card should list your name, current address and telephone number, major, expected graduation date, and the university you attend. You can tailor your own business card any way you like, as long as you include essential information.

You can buy business card forms at business supply stores like Office Depot and Staples. Using these forms, you can print your business cards on your printer. Then, as changes in your address, telephone number, or graduation date occur, you can create new business cards and print them in minutes, rather than wait hours or days.

Marianne N. Ragins

Florida Agricultural and Mechanical University Undergraduate Student
Graduation: April 2025
Major: Business Administration
Degree: Bachelor of Science
http://www.linkedin.com/in/marianneragins

Permanent Address
P. O. Box 176
Centreville, Virginia 20122
(478) 555-1212

University Address
FAMU Box 00000
Tallahassee, Florida 32307
(850) 555-1212

Résumés

Your résumé is one of the most essential networking tools you can have. A résumé is a summary of your education, activities, and experiences in a concise format (most experts recommend no more than one page). Most companies considering you for employment will require one from you at some point, so keep your résumé updated. A résumé is also often required when you are applying for internships, summer jobs, co-ops, or even participating in contests. Refer to the samples of my résumés in chapter one.

Résumés can be professionally prepared and printed by a print shop such as FedEx Office, or you can use a computer, laser printer, and heavy bonded paper to create your own. Printing your own résumé allows you flexibility to make frequent changes. It also saves money, as having them professionally printed is very expensive, especially if you frequently make changes. Be careful to purchase envelopes in a corresponding color and weight for mailing your résumé.

Cover Letter

Prepare a cover letter summarizing the key points and highlights of your résumé. You will use your cover letter when mailing or e-mailing your résumé to corporate recruiters and job contacts. The purpose of the cover letter is to intrigue the reader enough to look at the résumé you have included and to explain the reason you are writing.

In your cover letter, identify a specific position you are interested in at the company. Tie your qualifications and background to the position. For example, if you are interested in the position of market research specialist at XYZ Company, you would highlight your position as vice president of your campus's chapter of the American Marketing Association or relevant courses you have taken, such as Principles of Marketing I and II or Marketing Management.

Introductory Letters

Introductory letters are basically let's-get-acquainted letters. They can be used in place of a cover letter to familiarize a particular contact with your name and qualifications. An introductory letter is less specific than a cover letter. In your cover letter you should be specific about the position you are interested in and your qualifications for it. An introductory letter need only identify major areas such as marketing, finance, or sales, as shown in the introductory letter example on previous pages. An introductory letter can be also be written to a graduate school in which you're interested.

You may not receive a written reply right away, but if you communicate once a year, pretty soon they'll start to remember your name, your résumé, and your letters. If you reinforce this by introducing yourself at receptions and career fairs, you will create an even more memorable impression. Bing Spitler, former manager of college and university relations at Armstrong World Industries, explains: "Not enough students come to receptions and career fairs as freshman and sophomores. They all wait until senior year or the end of their junior year to approach us and inquire about jobs. If they were to get acquainted with us earlier, it would give us time to establish a relationship and learn of each student's progress and accomplishments throughout their college career. It could give them an edge over other prospects. In my opinion, college students should focus on the job, not the degree."

Follow-up Letters

A follow-up letter such as the one shown earlier in the chapter is another essential networking tool. Because one of the main focuses of networking is to create a favorable and lasting impression, sending a letter to thank a contact for the time spent interviewing you, talking with you, or referring you to someone else, is just good manners. It also shows your sense of responsibility, maturity, and attention to detail. Most important, it keeps your name uppermost in the interviewer's mind and is a written reminder of your meeting. Also remember, a written letter is more memorable than an e-mail since so few actually take the time to write. However follow-up is key whether electronic or snail mail because many don't take the time to follow-up in any form.

Computerized Address Books and Contact Lists

You should maintain an address book or contact list of names and numbers in a spreadsheet program such as Microsoft Excel, and create mailing lists in a word processing program like Microsoft Word. You can also keep contact lists in your smart phone tablet, or in a program such as Microsoft Outlook. As you receive business cards and correspondence from contacts or obtain names and numbers of potential contacts from friends or relatives or even a magazine article, updating your contact list will be easy, and all the information will be in one central location for quick and easy reference. Using Microsoft Word, you can easily print your mailing list of names and addresses onto labels or envelopes.

UNIVERSITY HIGHLIGHT

The American University in Washington, D.C., is one university that delights students with an experiential experience encompassing the classroom, research and the real world in one incredible semester. With government internships and courses on over a dozen topics, students are immersed academically and socially in areas such as American politics, economic policy, and international business and trade. The university maintains a vast network of private, nonprofit, and government institutions. With this extensive network, the university is able to offer a wide range of subjects for its Washington Semester and co-op programs, which are open to students from other schools.

Students who participate in the Washington Semester Program can earn anywhere from twelve to sixteen credits, which can be transferred to their university. All students also enjoy the benefit of having frequent speakers many universities only dream of, such as General Colin Powell, former President Bill Clinton, and Ted Koppel. Can you imagine the contacts you could make by taking advantage of the wonderful opportunities at this university?

If you were in student government and in charge of arranging and organizing the booking of these speakers, for instance, or if you were involved in any of the extracurricular activities tied to organizing speakers, lectures, or the Washington semester and internship programs, the opportunities would be endless. Consider these: powerful contacts, in-depth knowledge of government, a network of friends who attend the Washington semester programs from universities all over the country, job opportunities, and experience and advice from the adjunct professors who work in Washington and find time to lecture on campus. The possibilities are endless.

For more information on the Washington Semester Program, visit http://www.american.edu and search for Washington Semester Program.

Introductory Letter

P. O. Box 176
Centreville, Virginia 20122

December 15, 2025

Susan Brown
Manager, College Relations
SC Johnson
1525 Howe Street
Racine, WI 53403-5011

Attention: *Susan Brown--Manager, College Relations*

I have read about *SC Johnson* and its excellent opportunities in several career related publications such as *Fortune's "100 Best Companies to Work For."* In addition, I recently met one of your current employees, *James Martin*, who suggested I contact you regarding a position with your company. I am very interested in working for *SC Johnson* after graduation. My career interests lie in the areas of sales, marketing, advertising, consulting, or corporate relations.

After careful consideration, I have determined that *SC Johnson* would offer a challenging environment for someone with my background. In addition, the business operations of *SC Johnson* will be enhanced by the skills that I have acquired during college and summer work experience. While majoring in business administration and concentrating in the areas of finance and accounting, I have obtained a broad liberal arts background that has been supplemented by my extensive endeavors in the areas of communication primarily through writing and public speaking. As you can see by my résumé, I have authored as well as published one book and written another published by Henry Holt and Company.

I believe in stretching my capabilities to their fullest extent not only through competition, but also in service. I have participated in several competitions, spoken to numerous youth and adult groups, and served as a member of several organizations. For example, I am the winner over $400,000 in scholarship awards. I have also been a member of the National Collegiate Honors Council, and the Southern Regional Collegiate Honors Council. Currently, I am the vice president of Junior Business Writing as well as the Chairperson for the Bernard D. Hendricks Undergraduate Honors Conference. I am also a member of the *2009 All-USA Academic Team*. Furthermore, while participating in the aforementioned activities as well as many others, I have maintained a 3.8 grade point average and have been on the National Dean's List for the past 3.5 years.

Through these and many other activities I have developed extensive analytical, organizational, and communication skills. Therefore, I am certain that I would be a valuable asset to your organization.

My résumé is enclosed for your review. I would like to speak with you further about my qualifications and how they might meet your needs. If you wish to establish contact by phone, the number is *(850) 555-1212.*

Sincerely,

Marianne N. Ragins

This letter was originally written for another company by Marianne Ragins during her college years. Names, dates, and other text shown in italics are fictitious or have been changed. Marianne Ragins was a member of the 1995 All-USA Academic Team.

The above type of letter can also be used as an introductory letter to the admissions director at a graduate school.

Follow-up Letter

P.O. Box 176
Centreville, Virginia 20122

February 18, 2025

Brian H. Standish
Group Controller
Government Contract Accounting
3M Center Building
St. Paul, MN 55144-1000

Dear Mr. Standish:

Thank you for a pleasant and informative interview on Wednesday, February 19, 2025. During the course of our conversation I obtained considerable insight about 3M and its controller division. I am very pleased about the interview and after reading the information you gave me upon its completion, I am even more convinced that an internship experience with your company would be an excellent opportunity. Not only could I gain significant knowledge through the experience, I have many skills which 3M could utilize as well, particularly my complementing aptitudes for using existing computer skills and swiftly acquiring new ones.

Again, thank you for the interview. I hope that you had a rewarding and enjoyable recruiting experience at Florida A & M University's School of Business and Industry. I look forward to hearing from you soon.

Sincerely,

Marianne N. Ragins

This letter was originally written for another company by Marianne Ragins during her college years. Names, dates, and other text shown in italics are fictitious or have been changed. Please note that this letter was written and sent within one day of the actual interview. Follow-up letters should be written immediately following your interview.

Thank You Letter

P. O. Box 176
Centreville, Virginia 20122

March 5, 2025

Cheryl K. Hunt
Armstrong World Industries
Manager, College Recruiting
Organization Development
P.O. Box 3001
Lancaster, PA 17604

Dear Ms. Hunt:

Thank you for taking the time to speak with me on *Tuesday, March 4, 2025*. That interview was one of the most enjoyable that I have ever had. Even though you had an extremely long day with numerous interviews, you were enthusiastic and energetic throughout the interview. Anyone who did not have an enthusiasm for sales would definitely have one after talking with you.

I am convinced that Armstrong is exactly the place for me. I am very interested in an internship position in the sales and marketing area. The extensive communication skills which I have obtained as well as my aptitudes for flexibility and creativity should definitely enhance the operations of Armstrong. I have read about your company in the book, *100 Best Companies to Work for In America*. Armstrong is obviously an impressive company with impressive employees and products.

Once again, thank you for the interview. I hope that you had a rewarding and enjoyable recruiting experience at Florida A & M University's School of Business and Industry. Hopefully, your cold has improved by now. I look forward to hearing from you soon.

Sincerely,

Marianne N. Ragins

This letter was originally written for another company by Marianne Ragins during her college years. Names, dates, and other text shown in italics are fictitious or may have been changed. Please note that this letter was written and sent within one day of the actual interview. Follow-up letters should be written immediately following your interview.

Networking Sources

Alumni organizations
Associations
Books and magazines
Career center
Career fairs
Churches and other religious organizations
Civic and philanthropic organizations
Classes
Directories
Friends
Graduate and professional school days
Online databases
Professors
Receptions
Special interest groups
Sororities and fraternities
Social media (LinkedIn is a necessity)

Developing Interpersonal Skills

Developing good interpersonal skills is an important factor in successful networking and your professional development. Interpersonal skills are soft skills that most people overlook, avoid, or just don't take the time to develop. They involve the arts of writing, speaking, leadership, and related skills that can aid you tremendously in both your career and your life. They all revolve around communication and its place in your life on campus and beyond. Effective communication is one of the keys to getting what you want out of life. In most careers, it is an essential ingredient for success. If you cannot relate your ideas, stimulate understanding in others, or motivate people–including yourself–to act, you may have a difficult time realizing visions of success.

Oratorical Skills

Learning to speak in public without twisting your tongue in knots, coming up with ways to avoid the task, or panicking is important. In today's increasingly competitive job environment, public speaking is one of the most required skills, yet it is one that people most frequently avoid developing. If you learn to do it now, you will never regret it. It will help you in day-to-day conversations, in interviews, in business, in graduate school, and in many other areas of your life; and the more you practice, the easier it will become.

To develop your oratorical or speaking skills, you should take every opportunity in college to make oral presentations, participate in oratorical contests, and engage in debates. In essence, open your mouth every chance you have (as long as it doesn't get you in trouble!). Colleges and universities are notorious for the numbers of student rallies, protest, debates, discussions, and forums they have, so your campus is one of the best places to air your ideas and thoughts.

You should have many opportunities to learn effective speaking skills in college. In many classes, oral presentations are required. Unfortunately, many students avoid making presentations if they possibly can, just as some avoid English 101 or biology if they can. In our current society, the use of texting and electronic communication with smart phones, tablets, and other media has greatly hindered the development of speaking skills. So it is necessary to get continuous practice in classes throughout your college career to fully develop your speaking skills. Remember, practice makes almost perfect. If your regular classes do not require the oral presentation of material, you can always register for a class in public speaking or communication skills. If that still isn't enough, or you don't have the time for such a course, consider joining the debate team, literary guild, a performing arts group, or a mock trial team. All of these organizations involve activities that require you to stand in front of an audience and speak. To help you even more, attend workshops and seminars on public speaking.

The first rule of effective communication in the art of public speaking is to be comfortable in front of an audience, however large or small—after that the rest is easy. If you practice continuously in classes or organizations, you will eventually become comfortable enough to treat your audience as a collective mass of friends instead of having to resort to the sometimes unpleasant old trick of picturing them naked. The more comfortable you are, the more relaxed you will be, which in turn will allow your thoughts to flow from your mind in an interesting and convincing stream. It makes you a very effective and often entertaining speaker.

Writing Skills

In many of your classes, particularly those in literature or with a research focus, you will be able to find a plethora of opportunities to develop your writing skills. Term papers, essays, critical reviews, and analyses will be plentiful opportunities for you to practice writing. Not only that, many of your professors may also take the time to note major errors in your writing when reviewing your completed assignments.

Another way to improve your writing ability is to visit the writing center if your school maintains one. Many colleges and universities also offer classes on technical, business, and creative writing, as well as seminars and workshops to help students develop and perfect their writing skills. The University Writing Center at California State in Los Angeles is one example of writing assistance offered by a school to its students.

Interviewing Skills

Your campus is a great place to hone your interviewing skills. For almost every activity, contest, award, position, or job you will probably have an interview, whether formal or informal. As always, the more you do it, the easier it gets and the more relaxed you will be. Relaxation and practice are great cures for stuttering, forgetfulness, and roving eyes. If this isn't enough, visit your career center and sign up for an informational interview where you will meet with a recruiter and talk with her just as you would in a regular interview.

The only difference is both you and the interviewer understand the session is not intended to lead to a job.

Informational interviews are another form of networking. The career center will also arrange mock interviews with professionals in the office. Or you can attend workshops, seminars, webinars and mini-classes given by the center to aid students in the development of their interviewing skills. You could ask a professor or other faculty member–particularly one who has worked in the industry or field for which you will be interviewing–to practice interview you. Many of them will be more than happy to help, and this preparation will help you become more familiar with typical questions relative to that particular field or industry.

Also get prepared for interviews via chat and other tools such as Skype. There are some companies who may conduct initial interviews this way. For example, the Venetian Resort & Casino in Las Vegas, Nevada conducts some interviews for internships via Skype. Too, some companies are conducting "Twitterviews." They tweet an interview question, then look at your 140 character or less response to determine whether they want to proceed in the interview process with you.

Leadership Skills

Most graduate and professional schools *and* employers are interested in your ability to lead, motivate, and function within a team or cooperative environment. Joining organizations and obtaining a position of leadership is one of the best ways to develop such skills. As outlined in previous chapters such as "Life After Class," there are dozens of organizations to join, both on and off campus; and each, in turn, offer numerous leadership opportunities.

Some universities create structured student-run organizations and teach classes designed for professional development. In many classes, teamwork is very important. As a member of or a leader of a team formed in class, your leadership skills and ability to motivate others into wanting an "A" or some other goal are very important.

Many career centers sponsor leadership workshops, seminars, and classes to help you develop leadership skills.

UNIVERSITY HIGHLIGHT

Florida Agricultural and Mechanical University offers its students a wealth of opportunities in the area of professional development and enhancement. Many students can attest to the numerous internship opportunities all over the country, the various professional and interpersonal development programs, and other programs, such as summer research, sprinkled liberally all over the campus.

Students at the School of Business and Industry are immersed from the first day in a professional development program that encompasses speed reading, technical review and analysis of business periodicals, development of oratorical skills, business writing, and, most important, leadership skills. The leadership skills are developed and honed through active participation in student-run companies, many of which have ties to the "real" world.

16

The Student Entrepreneur

Budding entrepreneurs are on college campuses all over the world. You may even have an entrepreneurial bone hidden in your body. If you think about it, a college campus is one of the best places to start a fledging business. A campus is a tightly knit, concentrated world within which, with the right product or service, you have a receptive potential clientele. All you need is a good idea, the willingness to do a little work, and a friendly personality.

An entrepreneurial business venture in college could produce money to help pay for your tuition bill, your living expenses, a new car, investments for your future, a Christmas present for your significant other, or your dream trip to Hawaii. Your business could also show potential employers and graduate school admissions officers not only what an enterprising individual you are, but that you have initiative, maturity, responsibility, and innovativeness.

For a great idea geared to college students (individuals between the ages of seventeen and twenty-five), the college campus is a perfect, ready-made marketplace. Many students are eager to try new things, and because most of them are away from home and must find someone to provide various services cheaply, college is an excellent atmosphere for a low cost, low-overhead service business. Don't neglect a potential side market, composed of campus faculty and staff members and older college students. Although the older market may be less a target for you, it's never a good idea to automatically assume no interest.

In addition to an instant market, you have access to campus bulletin boards, dormitories, perhaps radio and TV stations, social media platforms connected with the university or college, friends who need and want to work, and professors willing and able to give advice.

You may also have the option of taking classes in entrepreneurship, marketing, advertising, financial and managerial accounting, the legal environment of business, commercial law, and so forth if you need additional information and development to run your new business. Some schools, such as George Mason University in Fairfax, Virginia, focus on entrepreneurship with special programs, alliances with the surrounding business community, and other resources.

Advertising & Promotion

Most colleges and universities have bulletin boards all over campus, the perfect place for budding entrepreneurs to tout their services or product. Or you may want to hang creative flyers on doorknobs to dorm rooms and faculty offices. On some campuses you may need to consult the student government office to make sure you can post flyers about your business. However, even if it is not permitted, a creative and agile mind can find alternatives for advertising the business.

For example, never underestimate the power of word-of-mouth advertising, which can be provided by your partners in the business, the people you hire to work for you, or the most effective of all, satisfied customers to whom you've given free services or samples of your product as a way of introducing your business.

On many campuses there are also radio stations, television stations, and newspapers. For a small fee or perhaps for free, you could advertise your business on one of those media. Don't be afraid to ask both the students who work there and their advisors, who are usually professors or individuals who have worked in the communications industry, for assistance in preparing your newspaper ad, broadcast message, or commercial.

The Internet and social media are also great ways to advertise your student run business and services. In most cases, they are also low cost ways to advertise.

Advice

Starting a business raises a lot of questions and issues. Since many of the professors on campus may already own or have started a business in the past, a lot of those questions can most likely be answered quickly and easily by visiting the office of such a professor. If he can't help, he will probably know someone who can. And if your business lasts throughout the year, many of the accounting and economics professors will gladly assist you in preparing your taxes.

If your business is successful enough to make a profit and reach one of your goals, such as paying tuition or the car note, and still leave you with enough for other purposes, certain professors are also good resources for advice on investment vehicles for your money. You may want to consider a class on investments or financial management.

Understanding Start-Up Costs and Other Issues for Your Business

If you have a product to sell, you may need money for the materials to produce it. There are several rules you should follow if you have a product-based business.

- Devise several ways to make the product. Research it thoroughly to find the most inexpensive way to create a quality product.
- Remember, time is also money! If it takes you a long time to make a product, you may want to reconsider your idea or approach.
- If you think your idea is really revolutionary, you may need to patent it or copyright it; at that point you should seek professional advice.
- Start small. Don't make more than one or two samples of the product.
- To advertise, show the items to friends and to staff and faculty members with whom you have a good relationship. If

they like it, word-of-mouth will help sell your product in the beginning.

- Get advance payment for orders. If you sell enough, you may be able to pay for production of a large amount. If your product requires outside suppliers, you may be able to get a discount for large orders—be sure to ask.

- Do not pay someone to help you unless you can afford it— until you show a profit, you probably can't. Your friends may help you for free as a favor or they could become your partners and share in both the expenses and the profits.

- Do not let your business, no matter how successful, overshadow the real reasons you're at college: to learn and have fun. Even though your business is a form of learning for you, you must remember you are in college and one of your major goals should be to graduate, which will be extremely hard to do if you don't go to class and forget to study. You must also remember to have fun. Don't fall into the trap of all work and no play. Not only is this dull and unsociable, it's unhealthy.

- Explore any legal requirements for your business.

If you have a service business, your start-up costs should be less than if you were manufacturing a product. You are the product. Since you are already made and finished, as it were, you do not need to pay for materials. However, you may need to pay for equipment to service your customers. For example, if you decide to offer manicures, you might need files, fingernail polish remover, polish, and so on. To advertise a service business, you may need to do a lot of work for free, since you do not have a physical product to show. Also, depending on the nature of your business, you may need business cards and flyers, which you can print yourself on a personal printer or have printed for a minimal fee at most print shops. After you've got these, you can go to work!

The following are some typical businesses students start on campus.

The Mini Beauty Salon

A mini beauty salon is fairly easy and low cost to set up. Consider the following example:

- Printing flyers for dormitory bulletin boards $30
- Facebook Page $0
- Equipment–nail files, buffing pads, polish, nails, etc. $50

Note: Before opening a salon, consult with the dorm counselor for regulations regarding this type of business—it may not be allowed on your campus.

Real Estate- Converting Homes to Student Apartments

This idea requires more capital. However, if your parents can help you obtain a mortgage and provide credit references, this is an excellent and viable idea. For example, depending upon the type of mortgage loan you can get as well as the housing costs in your area, you may be able to obtain a small, two or three bedroom home, townhome or condo with a low or no down payment and a manageable monthly mortgage payment that allows you to live in one of the rooms and rent out each of the extra rooms to other college students. Your rental income from the other students should allow you the freedom to pay utilities, taxes, and the mortgage for the house, and still provide a little extra income for you and your parents. After you graduate, you could keep the house as an investment and continue to rent it to students, or you could sell it.

This is a venture that must be carefully planned. First, look for a structurally sound home that will not require a lot of money to repair. If you plan to rent your house, you must make sure it meets the requirements of the local code officials for electricity, plumbing, heating, and gas.

Before purchasing a home as a rental, wait until you have attended the university for a year or more. This way you will know the town and its most desirable locations; will have some idea of the market value of the house in which you are interested; and will know the amount students would be willing to pay for a room in it.

If you're handy with tools and fixing things, be on the lookout for government auctions listed in the newspaper and on signs around town. Although many of these houses are fixer-uppers and some may be located in less desirable sections of the city, at some auctions you can buy a house for a minimal amount. Other ways to acquire an inexpensive house include VA repossessions, foreclosures, and houses on a realtor's list for over a year. Just bear in mind the costs you'll need to incur to make the house livable and legal.

Typing and Professional Services

You can help with a research paper, create a business card, proofread a short story, or polish a résumé. You can do any of these with programs such as Microsoft Word and a proficiency in English.

Storage Services

Several students on my campus, those who had apartments locally or were from the area, got together to provide storage services for students who lived far away and could not take their belongings home over the summer. This is an ideal and effortless moneymaker for students who have signed a long-term lease but may be leaving for the summer, or whose roommate is leaving.

Other Student Business Ideas

- Dating services
- Graphic designers
- Apartment locators and sublease finders
- Beauty consultant (for example with Mary Kay or Avon).

STUDENT HIGHLIGHT

Running down the field to catch the perfect pass or across center court to shoot the winning three-pointer was a way of life for Scott Price, an economics major at Florida Agricultural and Mechanical University (FAMU). As president and owner of Flagstik Productions, a small photography business, Scott was always a part of the action and poised to shoot—with his camera, of course. During his college career, Scott used his love of sports and photographer's eye to grow his business into a profitable enterprise. Even though Scott spent most of his time snapping pictures, he always found time for golf, his favorite sport. As a student, his photo business card, which he says is essential for the professional photographer, featured a picture of him playing golf and the slogan "possessing a photographer's eye with a golfer's touch."

Although he began taking pictures at the age of six, Scott didn't decide to use photography as a money-making vehicle until college, when he began working for two of FAMU's campus publications. While taking pictures for the Rattler Yearbook and the FAMUAN newspaper, Scott's pictures were noticed by an aspiring model who asked him to photograph her. When he presented the pictures to her, she was so pleased, she told others, who then approached Scott.

Seeing the power of his position as photographer for two major publications, Scott began to promote his business through them. For Scott, making contacts and positive word-of-mouth advertising were the key factors in his success. In his words, "It's not what you know, but who you know." In his sophomore year, Scott approached the FAMU Athletic Department and afterwards began shooting memorable sports moments and senior athlete portraits as the major focus of his business, although he continued to take pictures of aspiring models. One of his modeling pictures even appeared in *Jet* magazine for the beauty of the week photo. Still, Scott never rested. He also participated in photo contests. He won best photo of the month twice and a monetary prize in *U, The National College Magazine's* (http://www.colleges.com) photography contest.

Scott's business in a college town was profitable for many reasons. Scott explained: "Having two major universities in one city created a gigantic market of customers for me." Whenever he wanted to advertise, he posted flyers in all the dormitories and high student traffic areas, then distributed them by hand to people walking on campus. He also used other campus resources to his advantage. For instance, he appeared on *Snake Eyes*, FAMU's weekly television show. And in exchange for free photos of special athletic events, *The Capital Outlook*, a small local newspaper, ran his advertisements.

Why did Scott do it? "Although my business helped to pay a lot of my school expenses, my main goal for my income and the exposure from my photography was to fund and further my professional golfing career after college," he explained.

17

The College Investor

Wouldn't it be nice to graduate from college virtually debt free, or with at least a little money in the bank and a couple of investments on the side? Many of you who are burdened with student loans may feel this is impossible. But it is possible. In fact, it is quite probable, if you use the techniques of sound financial management. They may not make you wealthy and you may not totally be debt free, but at least you'll have some investments, perhaps a savings account, a couple of savings bonds, and maybe a mutual fund account or a certificate of deposit (CD). Even as a college student on a very tight budget, you can save a little money, have a decent size bank account, and maybe enough left over to try a few conservative investments.

First you need a little money. Let's think about it. The average fast food order is approximately $7. If you eat at a fast food restaurant an average of three times a week, it comes to twelve times per month (assuming four weeks in a month), or approximately 144 times a year—that's $1,008 a year spent just for food. If you gave in to only one fast food craving per week, you would spend $336 in a year. In Tallahassee, where I went to college, there were at least three coupon books sent to students every week filled with coupons for Burger King, McDonald's, haircuts, and many other items.

You could use the $14 per week ($56 per month) you save avoiding McDonald's, Burger King, and Taco Bell to accumulate $672 in savings by the end of the year. If you added another $25 dollars to your monthly savings, $6.25 per week, your savings would increase by $300, to give you a grand total of $972 at the end of one year. At the end of four years, without even investing your money, you would have saved $3,888! Not only that, if you get a summer job or paid internship, you can save even more money to invest.

Of course, you'd have to keep the money somewhere, so you might put it in a savings account at your bank. Interest is minimal and usually can be earned only if you maintain a certain balance, which varies by bank. Or you could wisely invest it in savings bonds, mutual funds, CDs, or stocks, discussed later in this and the next chapter. Or in the case of Dianna He, a student at the University of Pennsylvania (Wharton), you can open a Roth IRA. According to Dianna, "I am planning on opening a Roth IRA account soon to invest the money I'm earning from my internship this summer. What's great about a Roth IRA is that it's tax-free when you take your money out upon retirement." Consult http://www.bank rate.com or a certified financial planner for more information about Roth IRA's.

Let's consider your bank account, which could cost rather than earn you money if you don't shop around for the right one. Most banks charge fees and require minimum balances. Look for a bank with low or no fees. Otherwise, you could end up paying maintenance fees just to have the account, write checks, withdraw your money, or use an ATM. There are some banks–particularly in cities with a high percentage of college students–that will establish accounts specifically catering to student's needs. For example, they may not require a minimum balance, or they will allow you to write a limited number of checks per month or have unlimited use of their ATM, for a small monthly fee. You can also explore using a credit union.

Credit unions are nonprofit cooperative financial institutions operated exclusively for the benefit of their members. The credit union is usually composed of people in a group with a common feature, such as an employee group, geographical area, or those with the same religious background. The primary goal of the credit union is to not make a profit but to serve members. Many of them allow you to write unlimited checks and maintain a low balance in your checking and savings accounts, and they offer more money-saving options. If you are able to join a credit union, do so. If you or your parents belong to a credit union at home, you might be able to extend your membership to one in the city where your college is located. It will save you over the long run. To find a credit union near you, visit http://www.cuservicecenter.com.

Whether you use a bank or credit union, you should establish a good relationship with your financial institution while at college. Don't bounce checks *and* keep a reasonable balance well above the minimum required. Don't make frequent withdrawals. A good relationship will be helpful when you need loans (either business or car) and low-fee credit cards.

Now that we've found you some money to invest, let's discuss a few investment options.

Mutual Funds

What Are Mutual Funds?

Mutual funds are vehicles for people who don't have large amounts of money to invest. For as little as $500 or a $1,000, you can invest in a mutual fund. Some who opt for an automatic investment plan can invest for as little as $50 to $100 in mutual funds. Although the initial investment is much lower, participating in an automatic investment plan requires you to invest a certain amount every month. This amount is usually deducted electronically from your checking or savings account.

To establish a fund, mutual fund companies pool the monies of all the small investors and invest the total in numerous stocks and bonds, T-bills, and elsewhere. Each fund has a manager or group of managers who decide where to invest.

Depending on the type of investments the manager chooses, the fund can be classified as aggressive, aggressive growth, balanced, or conservative. Classifications are based on how risky the fund may be and the fluctuation in its worth. In simple terms, I think of it as how easily I could lose all the money I have invested.

The riskier and more aggressive the fund, the more your shares will probably grow in worth—or the more they may decrease in worth. A conservative fund will grow, but at a slow, steady rate and in smaller increments. An aggressive fund could grow rapidly and with wild fluctuations, plummeting one year and skyrocketing the next. With aggressive funds, there is usually a significant, steady increase over the long term (five to ten years), compared with small increases over the short term (three to five years) with conservative mutual funds.

As a young investor who has years before retirement, you may want to consider an aggressive fund. If you want to invest only for a few years (you think you may need the money after college, for instance), you'd do better with more conservative funds. Consult an investment professional for more information.

Terms You Should Know

- Load–A sales charge that can range anywhere from 2 to 10 percent. The load could be "front end," meaning you pay the charge when you purchase shares of a fund, or "back end," meaning you pay the charge when you sell shares of a fund. A "no-load" fund is free of the sales charges, but you may face other fees.

- Net asset value (N.A.V.)–The price of the fund per share minus the fund's expenses.

- Prospectus–A brochure or booklet containing information about the investment objectives, risks, fees, and management of a fund. This is a legal document and should be read by investors interested in purchasing shares of a fund before taking any action.

- Return–the percentage yield of your investment or its gain in value.

- Investment objectives–A description of the fund's investment plans and goals.

- Management fees–Fees a fund pays to its investment adviser or manager.

To get more general information about mutual funds or to find a fund in which to invest, visit Bankrate at http://www.bank rate.com, Motley Fool at http://www.fool.com or The Mutual Fund Education Alliance at http://www.mfea.com. Once you have determined how much you can afford to invest and where you'd like to invest, visit the fund's web site for a prospectus or call the 800-number. Read it thoroughly. Also, many books such as *Getting Started in Mutual Funds* by Alvin D. Hall are available to help you understand fully how mutual funds work. Peruse magazines such as *Fortune, Money, Kiplinger's Personal Finance, Forbes, Business Week,* and others to become an informed investor.

Saving Bonds

Saving bonds are a popular choice for investors with smaller amounts of money. They are easy to purchase and are usually available at any bank. They are obtainable for minimal amounts. Series EE bonds are available in denominations ranging from $25 to $10,000. They can be purchased in amounts to the penny. For example, you could purchase a bond for $36.50. Bonds earn a fixed rate of interest. You can obtain the current rate by visiting http://www.treasurydirect.gov. The interest you earn is added to the bond monthly and paid when you cash in the bond. You must hold the bond for at least one year to redeem and at least five years to redeem without a penalty.

Since the bonds are issued and backed by the U.S. government, they are a safe investment—you are essentially lending the government money and as such, your investment will *never* be worthless (unless the government is in jeopardy). If you want a safe, steady investment, savings bonds are for you. Although they will not make you rich quickly, they will help you to save money and deter you from spending it needlessly. If you bought a $25 savings bond monthly for four years, you would have saved $1,200, not including the interest the bonds accrue. Although it may not seem like a lot, it could be the down payment for a new car, or it could come in handy when you move to a new city.

Certificates of Deposit

If you happen to get a windfall of at least $500, you might consider buying a certificate of deposit (CD). A CD is a receipt issued by a bank for money placed in a special type of savings account for periods ranging from one month to ten years. Money invested in CDs usually gets a higher rate of interest than that in a regular savings account. The more money you invest and the longer you leave it in, the higher the interest rate will be on your money.

To find CD's, consult your bank or credit union. If you're interested in high yielding CD's and don't mind using an Internet based bank or one in another area of the country, visit http://www.bankrate.com.

18

Building A Blue-Chip Stock Portfolio On A College Student's Budget

It's been said for years: It takes money to make money. In most cases that's true, especially to make large amounts. However, with a little investment savvy, even college students who typically survive on a shoestring budget dictating minimal furniture, cheap dates, and endless boxes of macaroni and cheese can invest a little money in stocks. Even for students on scholarships or financial aid, there is money to be found for investment purposes if you really want to do it.

If you're telling yourself the author of this book is totally crazy because you have no money and can barely pay for school, then maybe you need to become an enterprising entrepreneur (see chapter 16) or maybe you should reassess your budget. You'll be surprised to see where some of your money is going without your realizing it. One of my friends and I looked at our spending habits for one month and discovered that 45 percent of our excess cash was going to fast food, the beauty parlor, and other luxuries. Read how to save just by cutting back on fast food in chapter 17.

To build your portfolio of blue-chip stocks you first need to thoroughly research the companies in which you are interested. For example, if you like drinking Coca-Cola or Pepsi, start by researching those companies; visit your campus or local library for their history and financial information. Or you can visit web sites such as Yahoo! Finance (http://finance.yahoo.com), Sharebuilder (http://www.share builder.com), or Motley Fool at http://www.fool.com for company research.

Assess each company's performance and earnings over a period of time (at least five years). Most important, look for information on each company's dividend reinvestment plan (DRIP) or optional cash purchase plan (OCP). You also need to look at each company's dividend payout and dividend growth potential. At this point, if a company doesn't have a DRIP, doesn't accept OCPs, and pays a minimal dividend with no growth potential, you do not want it on your list. As a college student on a tight budget, you may not be able to consistently purchase stocks of the company on the open market. You would have to do this if they don't accept OCPs. If they don't have a DRIP, then dividends you earn on the shares of stock you own will not be reinvested. Therefore, although your shares of stock may increase in value, they won't do it through dividends. Dividend earnings will be very important for your portfolio. To find the highest dividend paying stocks, visit http://www.dogsofthe dow.com.

Since most college students have little time to devote to continuous research and tracking stocks by the minute, trying to pick a stock that will grow by leaps and bounds in value is risky and time consuming. If you choose the stock of a well-established company with a record of paying dividends, you can invest and relax. Over time, these types of stocks have proven to be one of the most profitable investment choices for long term investors. Don't be alarmed by the rising and falling values of your stock. Invest, sit back, and hopefully watch it grow.

If you want to continue reinvesting in your portfolio, invest in the same amount at approximately the same time every month, quarter, or year; this is called a dollar cost averaging. A steady investment of the same amount at fixed intervals allows you to purchase more of your company's stock when it has decreased in value and less stock when it has increased in value. Over time, it all averages out and your investment should continue to grow.

Terms You Should Know

DRIP–DRIP is an acronym that stands for dividend reinvestment plan. A dividend reinvestment plan is offered by companies to allow their stockholder to reinvest dividend payments in additional shares of the company's stock. Dividend reinvestment is normally an inexpensive way of purchasing additional shares of company stock since the fees are usually lower or may be completely absorbed by the company.

OCP–OCP is an acronym for optional cash purchase or payment. This is when a shareholder purchases additional shares of company stock directly through the company.

Blue-chip stocks–These are high quality investments with lower risk than most average stocks in the market. Blue chips are usually stocks of companies with a long history of earnings and dividend payments. For example, IBM and Walt Disney are examples of blue-chip stocks.

Some companies, such as ExxonMobil (http://www.computer share.com/exxonmobil), have Shareholder Investment Plans (SIPs) or direct purchase programs allowing you to purchase your first share of stock and every share directly from the company. You must make an initial investment in the plan ranging anywhere from $40 to $500 or more.

If you want to diversify your portfolio immediately or the company in which you want to invest doesn't have a SIP or direct purchase program, you will have to use a broker to buy a minimum of one share of the company's stock. Most companies require an individual be a current holder of at least one share of stock before allowing him or her to participate in a DRIP or make an OCP.

Buying Through Discount Brokers

You can purchase one share of stock through discount or online brokers such as Sharebuilder.com (http://www.share builder.com), or TD Ameritrade (http://www.tdameritrade.com). To get more information about DRIP's and SIP's, read books such as *Buying Stocks Without a Broker* or *No-Load Stocks: How to Buy Your First Share & Every Share Directly from the Company–With No Broker's Fee* by Charles B. Carlson. You can also visit http://www.drip investor.com.

When you buy stock through a broker in order to qualify for a DRIP or SIP, ask the broker to register the stock in your name rather than in the street name. Registration in the street name means the stock you purchase is registered in the name of the brokerage firm rather than your name. Registration in your name, required for most companies' DRIPs, often carries a fee.

Once you have purchased one share of stock, there are quite a few companies that will allow you to enroll in their DRIPs. You can then buy stocks directly from the companies and completely bypass the stockbroker and the commissions they normally charge. Also, the companies who have DRIPs will reinvest the dividends you earn from their stock (see list below). This will eventually increase the value of your stock portfolios and could, given enough time, earn you another full share of the stock without your having to invest additional money from your pocket. Each year, you might be able to add stock from another company to diversify your portfolio.

Companies Allowing Direct Stock Purchases Without a Broker

This is an example listing. Other companies are available.

Procter & Gamble
Phone: (800) 742-6253
E-mail: Shareholders.IM@pg.com
Web Site: http://www.pg.com/investors/purchaseplan.jhtml
Initial Investment: $250

Exxon Corporation
Phone: (800) 252-1800
E-mail: exxonmobil@computershare.com
Web Site: http://www.computershare.com/exxonmobil
Initial Investment: $250

Johnson Controls

Web Site: http://www.johnsoncontrols.com (see investors, then stock purchase plan)
Phone: 1 (800) JCI-6220 or (414) 524-2363
E-mail: Shareholder.Services@jci.com
Initial Investment: $250

Dominion Resources
Web Site: https://www.dom.com/investors
Phone: (800) 552-4034
E-mail: Shareholder.Services@dom.com
Initial Investment: $40 (You are allowed 12 months from enrollment to invest enough to reach the required five-share minimum balance)

Unless otherwise noted, the companies listed above may allow a $50 or lower initial purchase if you sign up for an automatic monthly investment plan.

Investment Clubs

If you don't have enough money, you don't want to experiment with only your money, or just want a little company in your investment ventures, consider starting an investment club. Investment clubs are groups of people who pool their money like mutual fund investors and invest it collectively in stocks, bonds, and other investments.

Consider asking some of your campus buddies or even a professor to join you in an investment adventure. You can research and choose your investments as a group, have more funds to invest, and—with any luck—get a nice return on your investment. For more information on establishing an investment club, visit the National Association of Investors Corporation (NAIC) at http://www.better-investing.org.

19

Handling Credit Cards – Keys To Graduating With Little Or No Debt

Credit can be a nightmare or a blessing for college students. Whether you are freshman just starting or a senior on the way out, you need to be aware of your credit options. As a college student you have fairly easy access to a variety of credit and charge cards. However, due to the Credit Card Accountability, Responsibility and Disclosure (CARD) Act of 2009, if you are under the age of 21, you need to have a co-signer or show proof of independent income such as work study or a part-time job if you want to get approved for a card on your own. Even with this requirement, most students are able to get a credit card with minimal effort because some card companies will even count scholarships as a source of income. If you decide to get a card, be responsible! It can make a very big difference in your future financial prospects.

You should understand that building a good credit rating is essential in our credit-based economy, and a credit card is one of the best ways to do that. Responsible use of a credit card and the timely paying of your monthly bills are easy ways to establish an excellent credit report, which will cause companies of all types to rush to offer you services. On the flip side, if you abuse the privilege of having a credit card, it could haunt you for a long time and bring you a mountain of regrets.

Your credit report will be very important when you purchase your first car, get an apartment in the city where you find your dream job, get a loan for a super business opportunity, or, down the road, when you purchase your first home. Some prospective employers may even review your credit history, viewing it as a way to determine your maturity, responsibility, and preparation for doing a job. Having a bad credit history could destroy your chance at the job of your dreams.

Obtaining a credit card and building a good credit history will give you a jump start for managing your postgraduate financial life. During college, a credit card can come in handy when you have to buy a much-needed textbook for a difficult course or a suit for a very important job or internship interview but don't have cash on hand. There are many advantages to having credit and charge cards; however, it is essential that you use credit cards wisely and responsibly because they can quickly become a great disadvantage if misused.

Common Credit Card Mistakes

Common mistakes college students make with their credit cards and credit history are:

- Being enticed by the representatives credit card companies send to areas near your campus. Due to the Credit CARD Act, they must be at least 1000 feet away from the actual campus but the offers can still be attractive at this distance particularly if they set up where many students hang out or pass through. Many of these representatives set up booths with free offerings like candy bars, hats, tee-shirts, cups, two-liter bottles of soda, and so on. If you're hungry, thirsty or even bored after sitting through a two-hour lecture on ancient world history, these offerings of food and drink are often too good to resist. Your mind may have intelligently said, "No, you already have enough credit cards. If you get it, you might use it. You won't send it back," but your stomach wins with, "I'm hungry. I don't care. Feed me now!" Before you know it, you've signed up for another credit card and your stomach is happy and quiet for the moment. Tavia Evans, a Northwestern University graduate, comments: "After six years, I am still paying off these crazy credit cards I got in exchange for a t-shirt and a desk fan in college. Educate yourself about credit cards before you get one; check the APR; check if there's an annual fee. It may be helpful to start off with a secured credit card to teach yourself responsibility and then wean yourself off it gradually. Vow to pay off what you charge in less than thirty days. Keep one of your cards for emergencies only and try to keep the balance at zero."

- Succumbing to the idea of obtaining cash discounts offered by department stores for completing an application for one of their credit cards. This is usually a one-time discount and does not apply to future purchases. Department store credit cards have some of the highest interest rates. The annual percentage rate (APR) for most is at least 20 percent or higher. Since you can use a VISA, MasterCard, American Express, or Discover card at most department and other stores, stick with them. Department store credit cards usually don't offer as many services or incentives as major credit card companies and their issuing banks do. At most, they may offer free catalogs and advance notification of sales although some may have reward programs and frequent customer coupons. Also, having multiple inquiries for new cards on your credit history can damage your credit score and overall credit outlook.

- Being unaware of the terms under which the credit card is offered. For example, whether the card has an annual fee or not, the interest rate and its terms, and so on.

- Letting the ease of having a credit card cause you to indulge in overspending instead of comparison shopping or bargain hunting.

- Impulse buying of things you don't need just because the credit card is handy.

- Purchasing items on credit when cash is available. The student feels that he should have at least some cash handy, so he uses his credit card to keep the cash ready and available, not realizing that with a balance already on the card and a high interest rate, he could end up paying a lot more for the purchase than he would have with cash.

- Using a credit card for everyday expenditures (for example, using the card to pay the phone bill or the rent). Once a student starts using her cards for expenditures like these, they are probably digging a very big and black financial hole. If you don't need to use it for this, don't. If you need the money, you may need to find another, less expensive source for a short-term loan. Alternatively, if you have a rewards card and the money available to pay the bill, then this could be a great way to build your credit card rewards. This works to your advantage only *if* you are not carrying a balance on the card and you pay the full balance of the credit card bill on-time each month.

- Not paying credit card bills on time.

- Having too many credit cards. Numerous credit cards can create greater exposure to theft and loss for most individuals. If your wallet or purse is stolen, you may be liable for at least $50 of the amount the thief charges on your card. Also, with too many cards you may not remember all the credit cards you actually have and all the account numbers so you can cancel and replace them. Of course there are now web sites and apps for your smart phone and tablet such as http://www.mint.com or https://check.me to help you keep track of your credit cards and other bills. But it's really best to limit the number of cards you have. Amy Crook, a graduate of Duke University, advises, "Don't get more than two credit cards and *never* charge anything to them unless you know you have that amount of cash *already* in your bank account. Too many students think, 'Oh, I'll be getting a paycheck soon, it'll be fine,' only to realize weeks later that their paycheck wasn't as large as they thought it'd be. Credit card debt is one of the easiest things to avoid and will save you so many headaches down the road."

One student I interviewed for this book had fifteen credit cards and a debt of more than $10,000. He had student loans outstanding that were payable approximately six months after he graduated. To put it simply, he was not in a good situation. By making mistakes like being easily enticed by offers from credit card companies and department stores, combined with the rest of the most common credit mistakes, he created a financial nightmare for himself.

In his freshman year he began to obtain all types of credit cards, mainly to take advantage of the gifts, promotions, and cash discounts representatives were offering. He ended up with five major credit cards, including a Discover card, two Visas, and a MasterCard; five department store cards including those from Sears, JCPenney, Macy's and Hecht's; and five gas cards, including Shell and Exxon.

All of the cards carried a balance and interest rates ranging from 17.9 percent to over 25 percent APR. All of the major credit cards had low introductory variable interest rates designed just for students. But after one year, most of them increased their interest rate, which is standard practice. When the economy and the prime rate started to rise, so did the interest rates. For him, most of them began to hover around 18 percent. Even though most of the remaining cards had fixed APRs, all of his rates were at least 20 percent. Some of the rates were higher due to cash advances he received.

This individual got into a major credit mess, which is going to haunt him for at least five years, or until he is able to pay off the high interest rate credit card debt. I hope you can see how this happened and how you can avoid and emerge from college debt free, or at least free of high interest rate credit card debt.

Terms and Fees You Should Know

- Annual percentage rate (APR)–This is the interest you will be charged yearly. It is usually broken into a monthly periodic rate. To calculate the amount of interest you are paying when you make a payment, divide the APR by twelve to get the monthly periodic rate. Subtract the previous finance charges from your payment. Then multiply your balance subject to finance changes (which should be your previous balance less payments you made) by the monthly periodic rate. This gives you the actual amount you paid toward your balance. Most people who do this find the majority of their payment was eaten up in finance charges. For example, suppose you had a balance of $2,446.71. You make the minimum required payment of $50. Due to your interest rate, you have $37.28 in finance charges, so only $12.72 of the $50 paid actually goes to reduce your balance. This means the next month, your balance will be almost exactly the same, having been reduced only a fraction. In this instance, the balance was reduced only by 0.5 percent, or less that 1 percent. At this rate, it would take years to pay off the balance, and that's with no new purchases! Thanks to the Credit CARD Act of 2009 mentioned earlier, this should be easier to figure out because card issuers must include information on your statement about how long it will take you to pay off your balance if you make only minimum payments and how much you would need to pay each month to eliminate your balance in three years.

- Variable rate–This means your interest fluctuates with the prime rate. Depending on the national economy, your interest rate could move up or down. At times you could have a low interest rate, and at others your interest rate could be very high.

- Grace period–The period of time you have before your credit card company starts charging interest on your new purchases. If you carry a balance you don't have a grace period. New purchases are added to the old balance and interest begins to accrue immediately.

- Annual fee–Some companies charge you a yearly fee for the privilege of having their card in your possession. Even if you never use the card, you will still be charged the fee. To find low or no annual fee credit cards, consult http://www.bankrate.com.

- Cash advance fee–Fee for getting a cash advance (much like using an ATM) on your credit card. Most cash advances are assessed a higher annual percentage rate than regular purchases on the card. The company also begins charging interest from the day you receive the cash—there is no grace period. If possible, avoid cash advances.

- Company-issued credit card–Issued by individual organizations such as oil companies (Shell, ExxonMobil), major department stores (JC Penney, Macy's) and other retailers. These cards can be used only to purchase items at the issuing company. For example, your Macy's card can be used only at a Macy's or its affiliates. Most of these cards will allow you to make a minimum monthly payment on your total balance. This is called a revolving balance. Because most company-issued cards charge interest rates ranging from 18 percent to as high as 24 percent or more, carrying a balance with these cards can become very expensive.

- Travel and entertainment charge card (sometimes called convenience cards)–Cards that fall into this category are American Express, Diners Club, Carte Blanche, and the like. These cards usually allow you to have a high or unlimited credit line, based on your individual purchases, your ability to pay, and past expenditures. However, these cards usually require that your balance be paid in full within thirty days of the statement date. They do not charge interest during this period, but if the balance is not paid, they will charge a penalty, or a percentage of the balance due. The majority of these cards also offer additional features, such as product warranties and travel insurance. Most of them charge an annual fee. The best reason to have one of these cards is as a safeguard against overspending. If you *must* pay your bill in full when you receive the statement, then the temptation to buy something you cannot afford will not be as great and may even fade away as you face the possibility of a stiff penalty. Be careful! Some of these cards are now offering high interest rate extended payment plans for balances not paid off monthly.

- Third party credit cards–These cards are issued by financial institutions such as banks and credit unions, in association with Visa and MasterCard. They are the most common and widely used. These cards may or may not charge an annual fee. They allow revolving balances and have a wide range of interest rates, depending on the issuing institution. If you plan to pay off your balance in full each month, you won't have to worry about the interest rate. If you don't, find one with the lowest interest rate possible. To find low interest rate credit cards, visit http://www.bankrate.com.

It is also important to remember that credit cards allow you to purchase based on an established line of credit. You can carry a balance. Charge cards allow you only to "buy now, pay later." Later is when they send you the bill. You generally cannot carry a balance unless the card has a special feature allowing you to do so.

Credit and Charge Cards

Many major credit and charge card issuing organizations offer special student cards and often cater to college students by offering student focused reward programs and access to discounts with retailers. For example, some cards may offer reward points for maintaining good grades and paying your credit card bills in a timely manner.

You should definitely shop around for the credit or charge card that will best meet your needs. Ultimately, you want to have the least amount of credit cards to serve the greatest portion of your needs and make the smallest possible hole in your pocket in terms of interest and annual fees. Visit http://www.bankrate.com or http://www.cardoffers.com to obtain a listing of low interest rate and no-fee credit cards.

Your Credit Report

You should get a copy of your credit report every year–request it. Sometimes mistakes can be made by organizations that issue credit. They may report incorrect information to national credit reporting agencies such as Equifax and Experian. Monitoring your credit report can result in early detection of these mistakes; you can quickly clear them off your record. Doing so will ensure that when you need additional credit or a prospective employer checks your credit history, you will know it's in good shape. You can request a free copy of your credit report annually from each credit bureau by visiting http://www.annualcreditreport.com.

20

Student Loans and Your Future

Since applying for a loan can be much easier than researching and applying for scholarships, which typically involve a great deal of work and follow-up, most students turn immediately to a loan for their education. Many do not research the loan companies, their repayment terms, or the interest rates. Also students usually don't check to see if they qualify for a loan with the interest subsidized by the federal government.

The government will pay the interest on loans with subsidized interest while you're in school and for the first six months after you leave school. The government will also pay the interest if you qualify to have your payments deferred for a period of time.

On the other hand, unsubsidized loans may still have a six month grace period to pay after you graduate, but the interest begins to accrue as soon as you obtain the loan. This interest is added to the loan balance and will eventually increase the balance well beyond the original amount you borrowed. Unfortunately, many students are just glad to get the money they need and are happy to worry about the ever growing loan balance later or until absolutely necessary. This is a bad strategy.

Before You Borrow

You should thoroughly explore other financial aid opportunities such as scholarships, grants, and community service awards before you begin borrowing for college. Although many students will borrow some amount to fund their education, the amounts borrowed are often too much. Some will borrow well over $100,000 to finance their education.

While you're in college and not currently facing a huge loan payment, this may not seem like much. However when you graduate and you obtain your first job after college, handling a huge loan payment, a car payment, rent payment, food, clothing, gas, dry cleaning, and other miscellaneous expenses can be quite overwhelming. So it's best to borrow only when absolutely necessary.

To determine if you could be borrowing too much, I suggest putting together a budget for life after college. The budget should be based on how much you expect your starting salary to be in your chosen field. If you want to determine the amount your future loan payment might be for a particular amount you plan to borrow, use loan repayment calculators from the lending organization. For example, Sallie Mae, a provider of student loans and administrator of college savings plans, has a loan repayment calculator for the different types of loans they offer. Visit http://www.salliemae.com for more information.

You can find starting salaries in your field by visiting sites such as http://www.salary.com or http://www.bls.gov/ooh/ to review the *Occupational Outlook Handbook*. If the amount borrowed to fund your education will result in monthly loan payments consuming a large percentage of your future salary, making your budget unrealistic despite any adjustments, then the amount you plan to borrow is too much.

Indeed, friends of Janel Janiczek, a University of Pittsburgh graduate with a Bachelor of Science in Mathematics and a Master of Arts in Teaching, would agree. Janel comments: "I only took out the minimum to pay off. I have friends who graduated with over a hundred thousand dollars in loans. A starting salary of $32,000 with loan payments of over $800 a month doesn't leave much for other living expenses."

Alternative Ways of Paying off Education Loans

In addition to devoting a significant portion of your paycheck to pay off loans after you graduate, there a few other strategies you can use to help you pay off your education loans:

- Join the Upromise.com savings program in which you earn back a certain percentage from purchases you make at hundreds of online retailers. The money you earn back is placed in an Upromise savings account. Money in this account can be used to help pay off your education loans. See http://www.upromise.com for more information.

- You can volunteer or agree to work in an underrepresented area. Contact your state financial aid agency. Get more information about state financial aid agencies and volunteering to pay college bills in the 4th edition of *Winning Scholarships for College.*

- Consider scholarships and grants based on service to an organization. Some organizations will help with outstanding loans if you agree to work with them for a period of time before, during, or after your college career. See the chapter "Getting More Financial Aid to Finish College."

Why Credit Cards Are A Bad Idea for Funding An Education

If you're thinking of using a credit card to pay for your college tuition, DON'T. Unless you have a 0 percent offer from your credit card company that will last until you can pay your debt off, the interest rate on an education loan, either through the government or a lending agency such as Sallie Mae, is usually lower. Not only that, most education loans allow you to defer payment until you graduate or stop attending college. Credit cards generally do not.

21

Getting More Financial Aid to Finish College

Have you already started college and realized you need or want more money to finish? If your answer is yes, review the following tips for ways to get additional funding for your education. Students who are enrolled in a college or university often have a better chance at winning some scholarships, especially college/university sponsored scholarships, mainly because of close proximity to the source. In addition, undergraduates and graduate students have numerous chances to get involved in organizations and associations affiliated with their majors. Often these associations have scholarships available. The National Society of Professional Engineers and the National Association of Black Accountants are two such organizations.

- Look for scholarships and awards as soon as you know you may need more money. Even if you don't need additional funding, you can apply for merit scholarships, which don't require you to have financial need. Merit scholarships can look great on your résumé or curriculum vitae. But be careful! Some schools may reduce your financial aid package if you win an outside scholarship. If this happens, contact your financial office immediately to discuss your options.

- Review books such as *Winning Scholarships for College* and directories such as *Peterson's Guide to Scholarships, Grants and Prizes* for sources of financial aid.

- Consider entering contests such as writing, photography, and beauty that offer monetary awards.

- Visit web sites such as http://www.finaid.org, http://www.fast web.com, http://www.scholarshipworkshop.com, and http://

www.scholarships.com for information about scholarships and loan repayment programs.

- Speak with your academic department to get information about sources of non-need and need-based funding for students in your major.

- Contact the alumni association for your school in your hometown and ask if they offer scholarships or financial aid to students currently attending the school. Many often do, yet the funds are not heavily advertised.

- Contact church/religious, civic, and community organizations in your hometown and where your school is located. Many will help students by offering additional funds to keep them in school. Some also have scholarship programs for students in or from the area.

- Check with your advisor. They may be aware of funding opportunities available to you.

- See if you may be able to get work study in one of your school's on-campus offices.

- Research service scholarships for loan repayment possibilities. If you're willing to work for an organization either during, before, or after you graduate for a specified time period, you may be able to get help with outstanding student loans or current and future college bills. Organizations such as AmeriCorps and the U.S. Department of Homeland Security offer such programs. See the chapter, "Scholarships and Awards for Volunteering, Community Service & Work" in the 4th edition of *Winning Scholarships for College* for more information about these types of programs.

As a College Student in Search of Money to Complete Your Education – What's Different Between You and Other Students?

- *As a high school senior*—scholarships may be more abundant, particularly small amounts in the community.

- *As a college student currently enrolled*—undergraduate scholarships may not be as abundant, but you have the campus/community as a resource and can still search for funds based on your interests, major, or career goals.

- *As a transfer student* (from a two-year/community college)—undergraduate scholarships may not be as abundant, but you have the campus/community as a resource and can still search for funds based on your interests, major, or career goals. You also have the opportunity for transfer scholarships. Visit Phi Theta Kappa's list of institutions offering transfer scholarships at http://www.ptk.org (search for scholarships using the search function). College Fish (http://www.collegefish.org) is also a great resource for students transferring from two-year colleges to four-year institutions and the site includes information about college money for transfer students.

- *As a non-traditional student*—scholarships for adult students may also not be as abundant, but you still have the campus/community as a resource, just as currently enrolled students do. Non-traditional students should also revise their thinking. Search for scholarships targeting adult students as well as those for college students or college undergraduates.

- *For all students* - look for scholarships based on who you are, where you are, what you are, and your interests. For example, many organizations particularly those designed to serve a specific population (like women) could be an opportunity for you! So, if you are female, search for scholarships targeting women. Are you interested in culinary arts? If so, then search for scholarships targeting culinary arts. Are you a cancer survivor? If so, then search for scholarships intended for survivors of cancer.

As outlined above, you'll see there are many scholarships available, intended for all types of people. You just need to spend the time and expend the effort to find them.

Don't Make Assumptions With Your Search

Look at eligibility requirements carefully. A scholarship program may mention student classification but not age. For example, a scholarship directory or database may look like this one.

Council of Citizens with Low Vision International
Attn: Fred Scheigert Scholarship
324 S. Diamond Bar Blvd. #128
Diamond Bar, CA 91765
http://www.cclvi.org/scholarship.htm
Amount: $3000
        To qualify to receive a scholarship award, you must be:
- a full-time college/trade/vocational student for the upcoming academic year
- registered for at least 12 undergraduate units (9 graduate units)
- have a minimum cumulative 3.2 Grade Point Average (GPA)

As illustrated by the above example, the eligibility requirements do not mention age. The example above only mentions qualifications as they relate to your status in college.

Entries in books listing multitudes of scholarship and award opportunities might also include a category showing target applicants. For example, their entry might include a section such as this one:

Target Applicant:
- College student
- Graduate student
- Adult student

Once again, the entry above does not mention age; only classification. As a result, if you are a currently enrolled college student or a community college student transferring to a four-year institution, reviewing directories that include entries with target applicants such as the one above, could uncover several scholarship sources for you.

Associations and Other Membership Organizations Can Help Pay the Tuition Bills

To find associations and organizations in your area of study and check to see if any of them offer scholarships, look at the *Encyclopedia of Associations* published by Gale Research, which can usually be found at your local library. You can also visit the Internet

Public Library (http://http://www.ipl.org) and go to the special collections area to search for *Associations on the Net.*

This section is organized by category. For example, if you're looking for associations affiliated with engineering, you can go directly to that section. When I did this, I found the National Society of Professional Engineers (NSPE) web site as well as many others. I went to the NSPE web site and used their site search engine to search for scholarships. Using this method I found the $10,000 Paul H. Robbins, P.E., Honorary Scholarship for undergraduate students.

You can also use web search portals such as Yahoo! to search for organizations in your field. I used one of them to conduct an advanced Internet search, explained in chapter 7, for accounting societies and associations and found quite a few that offer scholarships. In the area of accounting, there were at least 6 organizations that offered scholarships. They included the National Society of Public Accountants, the American Institute of Certified Public Accountants, the American Accounting Association (AAA), the International Association of Hospitality Accountants (IAHA), the Institute of Management Accountants, and the American Society of Women Accountants. All of these organizations offered some type of accounting scholarship to students already enrolled in college.

Be aware—membership can definitely have its privileges. Some associations may require you to be a member of their organization to be eligible for a scholarship. Many others do not. For those requiring you to be a member, the membership fee is usually a smaller or reduced amount for currently enrolled students.

Other Sources and Ways to Find Money to Finish Your Education

- Magazines directed toward career and success-oriented people, such as *Money, Black Enterprise,* and *Fortune.*
- Try to get a paid internship. Many corporations sponsor internship programs for undergraduate and graduate students. Some of them will also sponsor scholarships for interns who have performed well academically. Even if they do not fund all or part

of the education of an intern, your job experience will enhance your résumé for future employment and scholarship consideration.

- Contact the athletic office if you participate in any type of sport. Athletic scholarships can be offered for many different athletic activities such as swimming, lacrosse, and tennis. To get a sports scholarship, you don't always have to play football, basketball, or baseball. Refer to the chapter, "Scholarships for the Unnoticed Athlete" in the 4th edition of *Winning Scholarships for College.*

- Contact the financial aid office at your college or university. Make sure to read your college or university catalog for a list of fellowships, endowments, and scholarships to get an advance idea of money for which you qualify. You should also visit the financial aid section of your school web site. It's best to have a good idea of the school's available student aid funds so you can ask specific and general questions about possible money to help you finish your education.

- If you participate and have a serious interest in activities such as music, dance, theatre, or art, contact the directors or departments for these activities to see if there are scholarships available to you in these areas.

- Review directories listing grants in specific areas to see if there might be aid opportunities that could apply to you. For example, check out the online directory *Foundation Grants to Individuals* or *The Foundation Directory* by visiting http://www.foundation center.org. You may also be able to obtain this directory in your local library.

- See if you may be eligible for an out of state-tuition waiver if you attend a public college or university out of your home state but still nearby.

- Try getting a company to sponsor you in exchange for your endorsement of their products or services.

- Consider cooperative education. With this option you may alternate attending school with extended periods of work for a company or agency that needs students in your area of study. This period could last from several months to a year. The company or agency you work for generally pays your tuition bill, or provides a salary designed to cover your tuition, in exchange for your services. In this arrangement your school may also give you academic credit based on the work experience you are accumulating in your field while working with the company or agency.

- Contact honor societies in your area of study – for example, engineering, and anthropology. Some may have scholarships and other awards available.

- Check out companies in need of future employees in your area or study or a related area. They may have funding to encourage your continued study in an area where they need future employees.

- Check with organizations that benefit certain groups to which you inherently belong (i.e. legally blind, women, minority, etc.)

- Contact your state financial aid agency.

- If you attend a United Negro College Fund (UNCF) college or university, visit http://www.uncf.org for information about numerous scholarships that may be available to you.

- Contact professionals who are already working in the field you are planning to enter or obtain your degree. Ask if they are aware of associations or organizations who could help you complete your education. For example, if you're studying in the field of veterinary medicine, contact a veterinarian. Alternatively, if it's anthropology, contact an anthropologist. Doing so may or may not help you find a scholarship opportunity, but it could get you a paid internship and/or valuable work experience which can help you win scholarships, grants, or open doors to other opportunities. You should do this in addition to trying to find national associations and organizations that may be listed in a book or have a web site, because professionals in your local area may know of smaller, community and regionally based organizations offering support to students. On social media sites such as Facebook or Twitter, search for associations affiliated with your field. For example if you're interested in a marketing career, you can input "marketing" into the search bar and see if any promising organizations are found. Reading a few Tweets or glancing at the Facebook page will give you an idea of whether the source you found may be helpful to you in your search.

Searching Locally for Funds to Finish Your Education

The local search is one most often ignored by the typical student. Many students in search of scholarships use a few scholarship directories and an Internet search service such as Fastweb.com which is wonderful but they need to go further. In some cases an Internet search service is the only resource used. Unfortunately if *your* scholarship quest includes directories and the Internet only or even just the Internet, you could be overlooking some valuable scholarship opportunities.

The best way to have a complete scholarship search is to search locally in your community, state, and region as well as using directories and the Internet. Most of the scholarships you find in directories and on the Internet are national which means if you apply, you are among many others who hope to win the scholarship. This makes winning the scholarship harder because it is more competitive. For many local scholarships the number of applications received from students is much smaller which makes them less competitive. This is probably because local scholarships are generally smaller in monetary value and a lot of students feel they aren't worth the time and effort. Fortunately smaller, easier to win scholarships, do add up and should definitely not be ignored. In my scholarship total of more than $400,000, awards as small as $50.00 were included.

For a local scholarship search, you should contact or review the following sources.

- The career center at your institution
- The department office for your major or your minor course of study

- Your current or university web site for special web pages listing scholarships that can be used at your school but are not specific to your institution. For example, Georgetown University has maintained a page listing outside scholarships for many years.

- Your college or university's site web site to become aware of scholarships, grants, and fellowships at the university specifically. Although you may not qualify currently, you may in the future if you can meet the requirements. Colleges and universities rarely keep track of whether students meet certain requirements in the future for a scholarship. You need to take charge of your scholarship quest by keeping track of your current and future scholarship eligibility at your institution.

- Community foundations. Visit http://www.novacf.org for an example of a community foundation and the types of scholarships a community foundation might offer. Do an advanced Internet search as explained in chapter 7 to find one in your area.

- Local clubs and organizations. Examples of these would be the Soroptimist Club, the Optimist Club, Exchange Clubs of America, Daughters of the American Revolution, YMCA/YWCA, the Kiwanis Club, the Rotary Club, the Lions Club, or the Knights of Columbus. Also look for sororities and fraternities. Alpha Kappa Alpha Educational Advancement Foundation (http://www.akaeaf.org) is an example of a foundation affiliated with a sorority that offers scholarships to benefit current college students.

- If employed, your company may offer tuition reimbursement. Contact the human resources department of your employer for more information.

- If you've interned with a company in the past or recently, you may be able to request financial assistance to complete your education. Some companies may automatically offer interns a scholarship once the program is completed.

- Companies and banks located in your community. Some may have scholarships available to local residents. Call the personnel or human resource department of these companies to inquire if they offer scholarships to students in the community. Your local newspaper or the Chamber of Commerce may be able to assist you with identifying local companies.

- Ask your parents to check with their employers. Some employers offer scholarships to children of their employees.
- If your parents belong to a work-related union, contact the union to find out if they offer scholarships to the children of their members. Union Plus is an example of a union that maintains a scholarship program.
- Contact any organization to which you or your parents belong, local or national, to determine whether they have a scholarship program for their members. Your church or faith related organization might be an example.
- Ask your professors and/or advisors. Some educators form groups to offer scholarships to students in special areas.
- Since some credit unions have scholarship opportunities for their members, you should also contact your credit union, if you have one.

Additional Funding Sources for Current College Students

Explore each of the following sections to find sources of aid to assist you with your continued education. Some are mentioned in earlier sections but here's a quick summary:

- Federal aid - Visit the Federal Student Aid section on the Department of Education's web site (http://www.ed.gov) to determine if you are eligible for any federal aid or grant programs.
- State aid - Find the organization in your state designated to administer funds for students who are residents of the state. For example, in Virginia, this organization is the State Council of Higher Education for Virginia (SCHEV). To find the education agency for your state, visit http://www.

schev.edu/highered/stateeducationagencies.asp. If this page is no longer available, search the web for "state higher education agency."

- <u>Membership organizations</u> - If you are a member of any organization on campus or in your community, contact the organization to determine if scholarships or general college funding is available to members. Your church or faith based organization is one example. Another example is the NAACP, a community based civic organization, that has scholarships available to its members and others. You should also contact your parents about organizations of which they may be members, since some organizations may have scholarships available to their members' children.

- <u>Scholastic Honor Societies</u> - Honor societies such as Golden Key International Honour Society (http://www.goldenkey.org) or Phi Theta Kappa (http://www.ptk.org) and many others have scholarships available to their members. There are hundreds of scholastic societies that cover interest areas from music to chemistry and beyond. Read chapter 10 to find out more about scholastic honor societies.

- <u>Associations</u> - Associations are a wonderful resource for students of all ages in the scholarship process to explore. There are thousands of associations in the United States. Moreover, many of them have scholarships available to students who want to continue their studies and pursue a career in their field or interest area.

22

I Am So Lonely Being Away From Home. What Can I Do?

For many college freshmen who are away from home for the very first time, it can get very lonely especially if they decide to attend a college without friends or family nearby. As I watched my family drive away leaving me behind during my first day on campus, I dissolved into tears. For the next three days I stayed in my room and didn't venture out except to attend classes or visit the cafeteria for takeout.

If the dormitory mother had not forced me out of my room to sit in the office with her, it would have taken me forever to make friends and join the social scene on campus. After leaving my room and sitting in her office for two hours helping students with minor requests and giving campus directions, I met two young ladies from my hometown and arranged an outing to watch our band rehearse.

If not for her kidnapping me from my room, it may have taken a while for me to start getting involved in campus life. Getting immediately involved in campus activities certainly helped Julia Rose Judge, a nursing student at Case Western Reserve University. She says, "When I arrived on campus, I took every opportunity to meet new people. I attended freshmen events, networked with older, experienced students, and soon enough I had a group of friends and mentors. I realized it was up to me not to feel lonely."

Being lonely can make you hate a college campus. It can even make you want to miss classes, sleep all day, stop eating, or even worse, dropout of college and return home. Loneliness happens to most students at one time or another. As long as you don't resign yourself to being lonely, there are ways to combat it and make friends for life or at the very least friends for a few hours or a few days. If you feel lonely, try doing any of the following:

- Get out of your room and comfort zone!
- Don't miss orientation for new students! For Hayley Ford attending new student orientation was a key factor in helping her combat loneliness on campus. She says, "The orientation program at my school (Marquette University) was amazing. I was forced to interact with so many other incoming freshmen, that on the first day of classes, I already knew a good chunk of my classmates. I also bonded early on with the girls on my floor, who are still my best friends to this day."
- Explore the campus.
- Join an association, club, or affinity group.
- Visit the student center or union.
- Talk to other students who seem to be lonely too. If you live in a dorm, open your door and keep it that way for a few hours. It could encourage others to stop by for a chat.
- Offer to tutor someone in your class
- Smile and say hello to those you meet.
- Ask questions of others even if you know the answer.
- Be interested in others (ask where they're from).
- Be productive.
- Call groups at home to see if anyone from your area is at the school. For example, contact any of the following:
  - Church or religious group
  - High school
  - Community group
  - Alumni association
- Visit common areas with a TV or games, such as your dormitory basement or a student lounge area.
- Volunteer! It will help keep your mind off your loneliness, give you an opportunity to meet other volunteers, add to your

student résumé, and hopefully make you feel good about your contributions.

- Go to the campus gym and exercise.
- Hang out in the dorm office where students come to ask questions or get key items.
- Get to know your resident advisor.
- Join a study group.
- Run for an office in student government. As you campaign, you will meet all types of students and others who may vote for you or help with your campaign. Also if you win a position in student government, most universities pay students a stipend for their service to the school.
- See if your university has clubs or organizations formed by a group of students from your area. For example, the university I attended had the DC Metro Club. It was a club composed of students from the Washington DC metropolitan area. This is a great way to make friends with those from a similar geographic area as yours. This can also be an easy way to make arrangements for a quick trip back home. If your school doesn't have a group like this, consider forming one yourself. Organizing a new group is an excellent way to meet people.
- Use social media such as Facebook or Twitter to find groups and other individuals you can get to know at your college or university
- As you meet others, ask if they play gaming apps such as *Words with Friends* or *Hanging with Friends*. Assuming you play also, connecting with others on your campus via this type of entertainment can be a quick way to engage them in a chat when you feel lonely. After you start the chat, perhaps you can meet face-to-face. This can help to combat your loneliness.

The most important tip to remember for combating loneliness is to get out of your room or apartment; go to a safe place or location where other students gather; be friendly; and start socializing! Daniel Lyons, a senior at the University of Missouri at Columbia offers this advice, "Every day is a new adventure ... if you make it one. There are students who hate college, but they are also the students who sit in their rooms and refuse to meet new people. Throw yourself out there. Meet new people. Join new clubs and sports teams. Not everything has to be career and study-oriented. Go out on a Wednesday night (so long as you don't have any upcoming tests or papers due). Do all you can to get ahead and stay ahead in terms of academics but realize that school work is only a chunk of college; the other chunk is whatever you want it to be. That's the beauty of college."

23

Top 10 College Pitfalls and Essential Tips for College Survival

The following are a few common pitfalls many students encounter and tips you can use for avoiding or handling them successfully.

1. **Pitfall:** Choosing a major based on someone else's wishes and staying in it until it results in your frustration and additional time to graduate.

    - *Tip:* Choose a major based on your needs and desires, not someone else's, including your parents or friends. Fraya Cohen, a Northeastern University graduate suggests, "Know what you're good at and use that to choose your major and coursework. Talk with professionals in the field before choosing a major. I knew a lot of people who wasted years in either the wrong classes or wrong major, and they wound up graduating in six or seven years instead of the usual four or five. Also, many friends of mine didn't know what to do after graduation. My advice would be to choose a long-term goal, like being a doctor, and then find out all of the steps you need to work toward that goal. Instead many of my friends and classmates started college undecided, took some classes in lots of areas, and then once they chose a major they were behind in the core curriculum, and they wound up graduating years after they were supposed to." Consult chapter 3 for tips on choosing a major.

2. **Pitfall:** Waiting until you're struggling in the middle or end of the semester to ask for help or visit your professor.

- *Tip:* Ask for help before you need it. If you know you are in a class that involves a subject in which you typically struggle, start asking for help as soon as class starts. Or if you take the first exam and your grade is dismal, go directly to your professor's office for a visit during their office hours. See chapter 4 for more information.

3. **Pitfall:** Taking too few or too many hours; not knowing where you are in terms of your schedule and path to graduation; and changing your major too late or too often.

    - *Tip:* Create a plan that outlines your path to graduation as soon as you declare a major. Stick to the plan and periodically conduct your own degree audit. Review chapter 5 to learn how to create your graduation plan.

4. **Pitfall:** Not managing your time wisely.

    - *Tip:* This is one of the biggest problem areas for college students. College campuses and being away from home can offer loads of wonderful freedom. And, most students love it. Unfortunately freedom can also lead to missed classes, missed opportunities, and poor grades. Develop good study habits, create a plan for graduation, and limit partying to only what you can safely handle while still being able to do well in your classes. Chapter 5 and chapter 6 can help you in these areas. Ryan Upshaw, a graduate student the University of Mississippi offers this advice, "DO NOT PROCRASTINATE! That's it. Give yourself enough time to really learn and absorb information, not cram it in at 4:00 a.m. when you have an 8:00 a.m. exam."

5. **Pitfall:** Partying TOO much and trusting too easily.

    - *Tip:* Having fun in college is certainly okay. However your pursuit of fun should be well balanced with your pursuit of an education. And, you should always be safe and careful about whom you decide to trust on campus, because some activities can get you into loads of trouble. Learn about your campus and the fun pastimes before you decide to become involved or hang out. Talk to recent graduates or others you trust who've been around and can tell you the ropes to skip and the ropes to know for your campus and college town. For Daniel Lyons, a student at the University of Missouri in Columbia, the biggest college pitfall is, "Alcohol at parties, plain and simple. There will always be parties every night of the week. . . . Parties are your best and worst friend. A great party can introduce you to some wonderful people and memorable experiences, but a party can also get you in trouble . . . You must realize academics come first. If you can go out every night and still score 'A's' in all of your classes, more power to you. But 99.99 percent of students can't do that. Remember why you're at college—for an education. Remembering this fact will be worthwhile when you're negotiating your first major salary, since your increased studying and decreased partying could make you even more attractive to future employers due to higher grades." Erin Husbands, a student at Louisiana State University (LSU) in Baton Rouge agrees, "At LSU, football and sports in general are a huge distraction. For LSU students, it's well known that GPAs are ever so slightly decreased during football season. GPAs always rise again in the spring. You also have to be careful during your first semester away from home. Everything's new—no parents, your own rules, and possibly your parent's credit card. You're eighteen and old enough to go out–which you will because now you can. Thursday is always a big 'going out' night and often you'll notice classes dwindling on Friday's lecture. While being on your own is a wonderful experience, you have to exercise self-control and remember why you're there—for school, not for being the new college bar guide." Refer to chapter 10 for more about life after class.

6. **Pitfall:** Letting loneliness overcome you and not getting help for your problems.

   - *Tip:* If you have a problem, let someone know. Either consult your counseling office or in the example of one student interviewed for this book, who had extreme test anxiety, contact your office of Disability Services. They may be able to develop a plan for you to work with your professors and get help with your classes, taking tests, or any other areas of concern. Read chapter 22 for strategies to help you overcome loneliness or chapter 2 for help with other issues.

7. **Pitfall:** Letting relationships, especially romantic relationships, rule your college life.

   - *Tip:* Love is wonderful! Indeed, many students find husbands and wives on campus. If you do have a romantic relationship, don't let it detract from your graduation plan or your ability to take advantage of all the opportunities that your university or college has to offer, including study abroad, internships, and other extracurricular activities. Tavia Evans Gilchrist, a Northwestern University grad, offers more advice on the biggest relationship oriented pitfalls: "The biggest college pitfalls that could get you off track while in college are getting pregnant, getting involved with the wrong crowd (of people), having a time consuming boyfriend or partner, and being too disconnected from campus life with a part-time or full-time job *or* activities that are not connected or even affiliated with school." Read chapter 10 for more information about life after class.

8. **Pitfall:** Not knowing how to handle credit cards.

- *Tip:* Don't treat credit cards like cash. If you don't have the money to pay the entire bill or most of it at the end of the month, don't buy. Don't get multiple credit cards as this can leave you open to too many fraudulent charges should they ever get stolen. Always pay more than the minimum. Understand credit card interest and how it is calculated so you will know the impact of carrying a balance and may think twice about buying unnecessary purchases. Even though it is not as easy as it used to be for college students to get credit cards, many can still do so if they show evidence of a job or student income such as work study. If you get a credit card, use it wisely. Consult chapter 19 for help with understanding how to handle credit cards.

9. **Pitfall:** Racking up students loans without thinking about the effect they may have on your future life.
   - *Tip:* Some students love the idea of a college and the idea of a major so much they rack up multiple student loans to stay at the school or in the major without any thought to the future or the total cost. Consider your future salary and the impact a huge student loan balance could have on your life. There are many college graduates who are still paying student loans ten or more years after they graduate. Review the chapter "Student Loans and Your Future" for more information.

10. **Pitfall:** Waiting until college costs MUST be paid.
    - *Tip:* If you know your funding runs out by the beginning of your junior year; or if your parents have told you they only have a certain amount for your college education and the school you plan to attend will exceed that amount; or, if you have a sibling who is about to enter school in two years and you know your parents may have trouble continuing to pay your tuition in addition to that of your brother or sister, do not wait until the college bill is due

and then be forced into a getting a loan or worse dropping out. Start researching scholarships and alternative sources of funding as soon as you know additional college costs that won't be covered are a possibility. For many scholarships and grants, you need to apply well in advance of when the money is needed. For example, the deadline to apply may be in October of your sophomore year. However, if you win the scholarship or grant it may not be credited to your student account until the August of your junior year. See chapter 21 and chapter 9 for more information about getting more college financial aid and entering contests and competitions that offer monetary awards.

24

Social Media – Can It Help Or Hurt Your College Life?

Depending upon how it's used, social media can be a curse or a blessing for college students particularly as it relates to your career aspirations or great opportunities. If used wisely, your Facebook account and public portions of a page can reaffirm a prospective employer's belief in your qualifications as a candidate. Or it can help them eliminate you from a huge applicant pool they're hoping to manage in any way they can. Also a LinkedIn page can be essential to a job or internship search because so many employers expect to see one for employment candidates.

Social media can be a boon to your personal life by helping you to stay connected to those who make you feel good about yourself and your place in the world. Or your use of Facebook and other social media can be a negative distraction that can pull you away from studies and face to face interaction.

The following are a few tips to help you manage your social media life:

- Use Twitter, Facebook and LinkedIn to help build your network, research careers, and uncover unofficial job leads. If you decide to use any of them in this manner, make sure your communications are professional and your postings and comments reflect your professionalism. You should assume that any information you submit can be seen by anyone (this includes via Facebook, Twitter and other social media). If you want something to stay private, do not submit or transmit. This includes personal information. And always be aware of the words you use and how they might appear to someone else especially if you want them to launch your career, admit you to a graduate school or contribute to funding your education. If they do not feel you will present a positive image for their organization, then they do not want to select you.

- Clean up your social media life. If your name and information is on a Facebook page, Twitter account, or YouTube video with derogatory, unflattering or inflammatory remarks, clean it up. There are many prospective employers and others associated with great opportunities you might be seeking who will search for you. You don't want them to find something negative that could result in them denying you an opportunity

- Use social media to find scholarships and college aid - increasingly there are many organizations that use Facebook pages, Twitter handles, YouTube videos and other forms of social media to assist students with their college and college funding search. If you want to determine if a program has a social media presence, you can use the search toolbar in Facebook (www.face book.com) to find their Facebook page if one is available. Just type in the name and see what comes up. YouTube (www.youtube.com) has a similar search toolbar you can use to find a program. For Twitter (www.twitter.com), use Google and type in the program name along with Twitter to see if there is a handle for them.

- Specifically, social media can help you in the following ways as it relates to scholarships, college aid and jobs:
    - If you like certain pages for scholarship and college related programs on Facebook, you may get alerts on scholarship application availability, deadlines, tips, and more. This can also work for alerts on job opportunities.
    - Following programs on Twitter might also keep you aware of tips, deadline extensions, application availability, and announcements.

- Viewing YouTube videos can help you understand a programs mission, values, and goals. This understanding can help you prepare for an essay or interview. Or, in the case of a competition, you may be able to view previous performances or submissions to help you prepare and perfect your own.

- Stay tuned to social media as a fun outlet. There are many events, contests and other fun activities that are announced via Facebook or Twitter.

- Don't let social media become a distraction from your studies and having a full college life. One of your primary goals should be to graduate with an awesome GPA, a wonderful job offer or graduate school placement, a few internships or study abroad opportunities under your belt and so much more. If you bury your head in your computer, tablet or smart phone for most of the precious minutes of your life, you will definitely miss out.

- Don't underestimate the value of face to face interaction. If most of your communication skills involve texting, tweeting, posting, and blogging, your interpersonal communication skills will start to suffer. This can cause a problem with interviews, oral presentations, team based activities, and other facets of your life. Being able to initiate and maintain eye contact with someone is important despite society's continuing reliance on technology for communication.

Jessica Kupferman, founder and host of *Lady Business Radio* has a wealth of information to share about the pitfalls and benefits of social media. Her tips are as follows:

- Use social media to round out your image as a young, fun-loving and responsible college student by posting photos of yourself volunteering, playing sports, and getting involved in on-campus activities.

- Start updating your status in full, grammatically-correct sentences instead of text-speak to show your proficiency in writing, humor, observation, and human kindness. In addition, when you start to update about subjects you are learning that you're really passionate about, whether it's biology, criminal law or cosmetology, you'll appear more knowledgeable in your field. And people will most certainly take notice!

- Many people on social media enjoy helping others. Debating an approach on a term paper? Not sure how to take the train to the city? Ask on Facebook and Twitter! Nothing makes people happier than helping out a college student. It makes us "established" adults feel as if we're contributing to your success, even in some small way. And this translates into adulthood, too! No one is more helpful than your social media connections. So take advantage of people's good nature and reach out in a pinch. You'll be surprised at the endless supply of resources at your fingertips.

- Whether online or face to face, gossiping and speaking badly about someone else rarely reflects well on you. Even "vagebooking," or, updating your Facebook status in a vague but still meaningful way, is transparent and makes you look like a "Bitter Bobby." If someone hurts your feelings, confide in your friends. Call mom or dad. But never lash out at someone in a public fashion.

- In general, it's better not to complain or be negative about where you work, other people's friends, religion or politics. When you are consistently negative on Facebook, people notice and judge you as a result.

- Lastly, revealing that you were drinking or doing anything you think makes you look "fun" now can really hurt your chances at a job or internship later. It's ok to be photographed with a drink in your hand, but it's not ok to be photographed as a sloppy or "out of control" drinker. See the difference?

- So are you wondering what you can actually say online? After all, you're human, right? Being tired, studying late, showing frustration over mistakes you've made, or displaying humility and your human side is generally acceptable. Just don't drag someone, someplace, or something through the mud. It's best to post about people, places and things you love as opposed to things you hate. And it makes you look like a really positive person to be around. Who wouldn't want to hire you then?

25

Top 10 Reasons You Should Get an Internship

Although internships are covered in an earlier chapter, I think it's important for a recap of the top 10 benefits of an internship, cooperative education position or some professional job experience before you graduate.

Those benefits are as follows:

1. Earn money for next year's tuition, books, fun, investments or savings.

2. Network and build your contact database for future opportunities.

3. Experience! Prospective employers prefer students who've gone beyond the classroom and gotten some type of experience.

4. You can get an immediate job offer. Many employers turn first to their pool of recent and past interns for new college hires. I received a job offer for permanent employment after college graduation *immediately after* I finished an internship in my junior year. I had one entire year to think about the job offer *and* to relax a little because I already had at least one offer of employment.

5. Your internship experience will help you become more competitive for scholarships, graduate school, awards, and other opportunities.

6. Your experience can help you solidify a new idea, product, or business that you can get started on as a college student or as a graduate.

7. With internships, you can make new friends, influential acquaintances and associates you can immediately add to your LinkedIn contacts, Facebook friends, and Twitter associates.

8. The internship can help you confirm your major and career interests.
9. The internship can help you explore a *new* major and career interest.
10. At the very least, your internship can help you learn at least one new skill *and* fill up white space on your résumé.

26

College Prep for High School Students

To help write this chapter, I asked a host of students from universities and colleges throughout the country several important questions about their college experiences. Read on and learn the ropes to skip and the ropes to know from college students and college graduates. Their answers will reveal to you tips for surviving and succeeding in college while also letting you know what they wish they knew before they entered college.

What I Wish I Knew Before I Entered College

Erin Elizabeth Husbands, a biological sciences and pre-med student at Louisiana State University responds:

- I wish I knew the enormous change in study habits I would need to make in comparison to high school. I used to study the night before, or rather memorize the notes given by the teacher, and take the test the next day. I didn't know how to properly study.

- I wish I knew time management in college would be very different. I had wonderful management of time in high school. However, time management became a huge problem my first semester. I wanted to participate in every organization and this just didn't work out. I was only able to handle a few, including my sorority, which took up a lot of time on its own.

- I wish someone had told me about ways to save money and cut corners in college. For example, no one told me that it was possible to get your book list before school started in order to save money and order books online. Or, if someone would have told me some classes actually don't require the book, or even that there are web sites for students to swap notes for classes.

- I wish I knew more about scheduling. When I got my schedule for my first semester, I wasn't aware that I could even switch my classes around. So I was stuck taking 7:30 a.m. classes Tuesdays and Thursdays all semester. That got old quick!

Julia Rose Judge, a senior nursing student at Case Western Reserve University answers:

- I wish I knew how to better manage my time.
- I wish I knew how difficult it would be to keep up with my laundry.
- I wish I knew I needed lots and lots of cleaning supplies for my dorm.
- I wish I knew my laptop would get every virus possible.
- I wish I knew how to better utilize campus resources, like the library.

Jordan Scarboro, a business administration and American studies major at the University of North Carolina at Chapel Hill says:

- I wish I knew you DO NOT need all of the stuff you bring!
- I wish I knew that sometimes it IS ok to say "no!"
- I wish I knew that the friends you choose become your family, so choose wisely and love them.

Tavia Evans Gilchrist, a Northwestern University graduate with a degree in journalism responds:

- I wish I knew I needed better study skills.
- I wish I knew you don't have to be involved in everything or join every group on campus.
- I wish someone had prepared me for the enigma that is black sororities and fraternities.
- I wish I knew how important it is to work hard to keep diverse friends in your social and study groups.

- I wish I knew how to find mentors among the good professors on campus.

Amelia Mehtar, a student at Case Western Reserve University, majoring in chemistry and Spanish replies:

- I wish I knew that it is okay not to be perfect. Upon entering college I was the typical over-achiever who was in every club, organization, sport, community service group, and was also able to excel in school and manage it all very well. Life was generally perfect. Upon entering college I found out that it is not worth being in every club and organization while only being partially dedicated to it and losing sleep to get good grades. I realized it is better to be really dedicated to a few things and do them to the best of your ability, rather than doing all of them poorly. This revelation to me seemed like a flaw and a glitch in my perfect record of being in every club. However, I realized being obsessed with this unattainable perfection was useless and being human and well-rounded was much more valuable.
- I wish I knew how small the dorm rooms were.
- I wish I knew how to manage time more effectively.
- I wish I knew how hard it would be on my mother to have me away from home.

Daniel Lyons, a student at the University of Missouri in Columbia, responds:

- I wish I knew you should apply for every scholarship possible.
- I wish I knew to take an immediate leadership role in organizations.
- I wish I knew if you wanted to be known on a major campus as a "doer," join the student government.

Roberto Lopez Jr., a law student at Baylor University, answers:

- I wish I knew what undergraduate advisors were.
- I wish I knew the format and process for graduate and law school admissions.

- I wish I knew about web sites to help me select classes and using Facebook to meet people before arriving on campus.
- I wish I knew the best places to eat around campus and about local nightlife.
- I wish I knew about Christian fraternities.

Ashley Chang, a business administration and broadcast journalism major at The University of Southern California, says:
- I wish I didn't bring so many things from home. Over the year, I accumulated even more clothes, school paraphernalia, books, etc…moving out was a nightmare!
- I wish I knew not to overestimate yourself and pick early classes when you know you are not a morning person! Waking up early in college somehow seems so much harder…
- I wish I knew that weird things happen in the laundry room … one time I found a pair of anonymously owned boxers (in my laundry…yuck!). But, if you ever run out of detergent or softener, it's nice to know your neighbor will probably lend you some (living in the dorms is awesome!).
- I wish I knew that aside from lengthy lectures and long nights spent studying or frantically essay-ing, the school year goes by so incredibly fast—make use of every moment (No joke. You will be astonished at how quickly time flies).
- I wish I knew that libraries and snack shacks open 24/7 are gifts from God.

Hodari Pilli Tourre Brown, a graduate from Tennessee State University answers:
- I wish I knew how important scholarships and grants are and to take care of financial aid as early as possible.
- I wish I knew more about student life and how students really interact on a college campus.
- I wish I knew that every person you meet isn't a good person for you.

- I wish I knew to seek guidance on all college decisions.

Deneige Kay Miles, a University of Mary graduate who attended graduate school at the University of North Carolina at Chapel Hill replies:
- I wish I knew that dorm life isn't always fun!
- I wish I knew that studying really does matter, regardless of how many people say it doesn't!
- I wish I knew that summer session is definitely not the same!

Jaime Cargill, a recent graduate from the University of Boise answers:
- I wish I knew not to sweat the small stuff—it will drive you nuts and take your attention off the stuff that matters.
- I wish I knew perfection is a great thought, but totally not practical. Be willing to make mistakes and then be smart enough to learn and grow from them.
- I wish I knew that what you were or who you think you are will be completely challenged in college. College is a perfect opportunity to search yourself and get to know what makes you tick.
- I wish I knew that college is meant to be educational, but you also need to have a little fun.
- I wish I knew people will have a million different opinions. You don't have to agree with them, but you also don't have to argue with them—differences really make college a great mixing pot where you can learn to appreciate others' opinions and value your own at the same time.

Finally, *Janice Hyllengren*, a college graduate with a B.A. from the University of Notre Dame and a doctorate from the University of Southern California urges:
- Don't procrastinate! Even if you were able to procrastinate a little bit in high school and it didn't come back to bite you in the butt, it will in college! Or, you will just stress yourself out when the stress could have been avoided. You will also learn

more and retain more if you don't procrastinate. Just do a certain amount of schoolwork each night, and you will be a much happier camper the night before an exam!

- Speak up in class. It is absolutely true that if you have a question about something the professor just said, there are definitely others in the class who have the same question. Don't be afraid to ask questions. Your classmates will thank you for it. The only dumb question is the one left unasked.

- In college, you are not just going to develop yourself intellectually, but also socially and emotionally. A lot of what you learn in college occurs outside of the classroom.

- Don't hurt people (like old boyfriends who you're not interested in anymore), because you'll regret it and may carry it with you for the rest of your life.

- Everyone feels the way you do—if you're lonely because your parents just dropped you off your freshman year, the other freshman feel the same way; if you feel overwhelmed about what is to come, other people are feeling the same way. Just go talk to somebody—you'll probably make a new friend!

Campus Advice from College Students and Recent Grads

Students who were still on the campus and recent graduates were also asked to share the most important advice they would give a high school student about preparing for college. Here's what they had to say.

Julia Rose Judge, a nursing student at Case Western Reserve University advises high school students preparing for college, "Before you go to college, make sure you are in the mindset to study, study, study. Many students realize too late that college tests are a lot more difficult than tests in high school."

Charity Avery, a junior at University of Tennessee suggests, "Prepare early. Get involved in organizations and volunteer work as a freshman. Take the ACT preparation and the actual test earlier than what is asked. Visit colleges during the summer . . ."

Spencer Blevins, a student at Gardner-Webb University comments, "Be involved in your community as well as your school. Keep a record of everything you do when you do it. You will never remember in your senior year things you did in your freshman year."

Daniel Lyons, a student at the University of Missouri in Columbia replies, "Get involved in as many things as possible—but only if you're truly passionate about them. You'll meet your best friends in the various organizations you become a part of. Also, find ways to stand out from your fellow classmates; the easiest way to do so is to start a new club, volunteer organization, or philanthropic effort, all of which will look great to future scholarship committees."

Jeannette Bennett, a computer science and electrical engineering graduate from the Massachusetts Institute of Technology suggests, "Work on time management skills. Learn how to balance social activities and academic commitments." Jeannette also advises, "Think BIG! Don't limit yourself when looking at colleges to attend, experiences to pursue, and careers to pursue. Don't reject them–let them reject you!"

Erin Elizabeth Husbands, a Louisiana State University student comments, "I would absolutely advise students to take every class that is important to their future. For example, I planned on majoring in pre-med, so I took all the biology, chemistry, and physics classes required and not required by my high school. I also took the ACT very early just to get a feel for the test and then I took a prep course to ensure that I would excel. Colleges also weigh involvement in extracurricular activities—so join everything and try to hold an office at one time within the organization. Also do other things to separate yourself from every other student applying—travel, take up interesting hobbies, and start new clubs. Oh and if you're going to do all this and still excel in school—get a secretary! My mom was my ever devoted fan and personal assistant!—Just kidding, we were a team!"

Roberto Lopez Jr., a graduate of the University of Texas in Austin comments, "Although it seems sad, do not choose a college based on the place where the majority of your friends will be going or its athletic successes, but rather the college that is known for educating the brightest in your future profession."

Keys to Preparing for College in High School

To get the best preparation for college in high school, you should focus on the following areas:

- Learn how to manage time wisely and avoid procrastination–This is one of the biggest pitfalls for college students. There are so many distractions and activities other than classes for a college student that managing time and staying on top of coursework will be incredibly difficult if you succumb to procrastination and don't manage your time wisely.
- Develop reading skills–In college, being able to get through several chapters in a book quickly and with comprehension will be very important.
- Hone your writing skills–Learning to get beyond writer's block and write well is important not only in college but also for winning scholarships to attend or finish college.
- Improve study skills–Excelling in classes will really depend on how well you can understand and retain information.
- Get involved in extracurricular activities–Colleges and scholarship programs are very interested in your activities beyond the classroom which help to differentiate you from others who may have similar grades and test scores.

- Immerse yourself in community service–Colleges and scholarship programs are interested in students who are committed to volunteer service and making a contribution to society.

- Explore interesting hobbies–College and scholarship programs look at well-rounded students. Selection committees and admissions officials are very interested in how you spend your time outside of high school.

- Participate in college tours–Visit colleges early. The largest and most competitive colleges and universities have the earliest deadlines for admissions and scholarship consideration. As a result, you need to know early in your senior year to which schools you're interested in applying.

- Enhance test taking skills–Most colleges and universities require an SAT or an ACT score report. Get prepared for these tests but also learn general test-taking skills so you can do well on final exams and mid-terms in college.

- Résumé writing and interview skills–For some scholarship programs you may need to interview or submit a résumé highlighting your activities. Not only that, these skills will be necessary in college as you prepare for internships, research, jobs, and other opportunities.

- Develop leadership skills–Scholarship programs and college campuses love student leaders. Attend seminars. Volunteer for leadership positions and initiate activities to develop and showcase your leadership capabilities.

- Identify strengths and weaknesses now–If you know how to recognize your strengths and weakness, you can create a plan of action for taking remedial courses, visiting study labs, and joining study groups in college.

- Clean up your social media life. If your name and information is on a Facebook page, Twitter account, or YouTube video with derogatory, unflattering or inflammatory remarks, clean it up. Although many outside scholarship programs may not have the time to look you up on social media, there are some programs that might AND there are many universities and colleges that will, particularly if they are considering whether to admit you and/or award one of the most prestigious scholarships they have to you.

- Get prepared for the scholarship search and application process early–The most competitive scholarship programs will have deadlines early in your senior year; for example in the months of October and November. To give yourself the best opportunity to win merit or need-based scholarships, you should start preparing as early as freshman year. Researching available scholarships, yearly deadlines, and the scholarship application process well before senior year will lessen some of the pressure to get everything done and allow you to fully enjoy your final year of high school. Also, you may be able to apply for scholarships, such as the Nordstrom or Kohl's scholarship, before you become a high school senior. See *Winning Scholarships for College* (4th edition) for more information about scholarships you can win from kindergarten to 11th grade. Also consider *The Scholarship Monthly Planner* from http://www.scholarshipworkshop.com to help you keep track of deadlines.

- Consider dual enrollment (if your high school offers it) or taking community college courses—Not only does this look great on your high school transcript, it can also help you when it comes to consideration for competitive scholarship competitions.

- Take Advanced Placement (AP), honors and other challenging courses—Doing so can help you prepare for collegiate level coursework. Also, certain scores on the AP exam can exempt you from taking some courses while at college.

- Become savvy with social media and online interviews. You could have a college or scholarship interview via Twitter (see

Twitterviews), Google Hangouts, or some other online or social media platform.

27

Final Thoughts

*A*ll *I Really Need to Know I Learned in Kindergarten* by Robert Fulghum hit home with many people. In my opinion, everything you need to know about life you'll learn in college—if you learned it in kindergarten, you'll learn it all over again. This time it will mean something, unlike when you were a six-year-old and your biggest worry was how to wheedle another chocolate chip cookie from your mother, or how to open up your presents before Christmas without your parents' finding out.

In college you will learn how to cooperate, commiserate, educate, manipulate, plead, grovel, laugh, and so much more. Everything you learn, good or bad, will enrich you as an adult and prepare you for the rest of your life's journey. Whether your experiences delight or disgust you, college is an overall educational experience. Make sure not to skip any part of it. No one likes disappointment and pain, but sometimes we all have to put up with both to experience life fully. If you work hard not only to survive your college years and graduate but also to get the most out of your college experiences, you will not be disappointed.

College should not be undertaken solely to get a degree—go to college to get an education by taking advantage of opportunities that can start you on the path to success. Many opportunities will lie directly in your path while you're in college. Watch out—opportunity could be knocking at your door at any moment. Common pitfalls could also be waiting to hinder your progress. Will you be ready?

For those who believe you should focus only on getting a degree, understand that the majority of college graduates don't work in the field in which they obtained their degree. Instead, they are usually in a field they happened on by accident or they nurtured as a sideline interest in college.

If you, the reader, use this book to help you get the most of your college experience and to survive the snags that sometimes accompany the college journey, you will enjoy a richer life, both during and after college. If you're thinking about going to college or are already in college, make the most of the experience. You won't regret it!

APPENDIX

Other Resources from Marianne Ragins

Books and Publications

The Scholarship & College Essay Planning Kit
- If you have trouble getting beyond a blank page when it comes to writing an essay, this resource is for you. This resource is updated yearly.

Get Money for College – An Audio Series
- If you don't have time to read a book or attend a class but you do have time to listen, this audio series can help you learn how to find and win scholarships for college.

10 Steps for Using the Internet in Your Scholarship Search
- This is a resource designed to be used at your computer to walk you step by step through using the Internet for your scholarship search. It keeps you from being overwhelmed by the massive amount of sometimes misleading information found on the web. This resource is updated yearly.

The Scholarship Monthly Planning Calendar
- This convenient and easy to use monthly planning calendar will help you with time management, getting organized, and staying on track with activities to meet major scholarship and award deadlines. This resource is updated yearly.

Winning Scholarships for College
- In *Winning Scholarships for College*, Marianne Ragins, the winner of more than $400,000 in scholarship funds, proves that it's not always the students with the best grades or the highest SAT scores who win scholarships. Whether you are in high school, returning to or currently enrolled in college, or planning to study abroad, this easy to follow college scholarship guide will show you the path to scholarship success. One of the most comprehensive books on winning scholarships and written by a successful scholarship recipient, it reveals where and how to search for funds, and walks you step by step through the scholarship application process.

Last Minute College Financing Guide

- If you've got the acceptance letter, but are still wondering how to pay the tuition bill because you haven't yet started searching for college money, this resource is for you!

Workshops & Boot Camps

The Scholarship Workshop Presentation

- In The Scholarship Workshop presentation which is a 1, 2, or 3 hour interactive seminar, speaker Marianne Ragins proves that it is not always the student with the best grades or the highest SAT scores who wins scholarships. Instead she shows students of all ages that most scholarships are awarded to students who exhibit the best preparation. By attending The Scholarship Workshop presentation, a student will be well prepared to meet the challenge of finding and winning scholarships. The presentation is designed to help students conduct a successful scholarship search from the research involved in finding scholarship money to the scholarship essays, scholarship interview tips and strategies involved in winning them. This presentation is usually sponsored by various organizations and individuals usually attend at no cost. Attendees of the presentation become eligible for the Ragins/Braswell National scholarship sponsored by Marianne. If you or your organization is interested in sponsoring a workshop or motivational presentation with Marianne Ragins, visit www.scholarshipworkshop.com.

The Scholarship Workshop Weekend Boot Camp

- This is an expanded version of The Scholarship Workshop presentation – It is a full day and a half of activities designed to help students and parents leave the weekend with scholarship essays, résumés, and applications completed and ready to go. The workshop weekend boot camp is usually sponsored by various organizations and individuals usually attend at no cost. Attendees of the presentation become eligible for the Ragins/Braswell National scholarship sponsored by Marianne. If you or your organization is interested in sponsoring a workshop or motivational presentation with Marianne Ragins, visit www.scholarshipworkshop.com.

Webinars & Online Classes

- *The Scholarship Class for High School Students and Their Parents*
- *Scholarship, Fellowship & Grant* Information Session *for Students Already in College, Returning to College, and Pursuing Graduate School*
  - The above classes are webinar versions of the Scholarship Workshop presentation. It is offered for those who do not live in

an area where a workshop is being sponsored. Attendees of either class become eligible for the Ragins/Braswell National Scholarship.

- *Writing Scholarship & College Essays for the Uneasy Student Writer – A Webinar*
- *Turbocharge Your Résumé - Résumé Writing Skills to Help You Stand Out from the Crowd – A Webinar*
- *Preparation Skills for Scholarship & College Interviews – A Webinar*
- *Minimizing College Costs and Student Loans – A Webinar*

For more information about webinars and online classes available, visit www.scholarshipworkshop.com/online-classes.

eBooks

Marianne Ragins also has numerous e-Books available for Nook, Kindle and iPad. Visit www.scholarshipworkshop.com/ebooks for the latest!

You can find information and additional resources from Marianne Ragins by visiting or connecting with her using the following:

- www.scholarshipworkshop.com
- www.facebook.com/scholarshipworkshop
- www.twitter.com/ScholarshipWork
- www.shop.scholarshipworkshop.com

About the Author

In her senior year of high school, Marianne Ragins won over $400,000 in scholarships for college. As perhaps the first student ever to amass nearly half a million dollars in scholarship money, she has been featured in many publications including *USA Today, People, Ebony, Newsweek, Money, Essence, Family Money, Black Enterprise* and on the cover of *Parade*. She has also made hundreds of radio and television appearances on shows such as "Good Morning America," "The Home Show," and the "Mike & Maty Show."

Marianne Ragins received a master of business administration (MBA) from George Washington University in Washington, DC and a bachelor of science (BS) degree in business administration from Florida Agricultural and Mechanical University in Tallahassee, Florida. Both degrees were entirely funded by scholarships and other free aid.

Marianne Ragins is also the author of the highly successful *Winning Scholarships for College: An Insider's Guide* and many other publications. She is an experienced motivational speaker and lecturer who has traveled nationally and internationally conducting The Scholarship Workshop presentation and giving other motivational seminars and speeches. Marianne is the publisher of www.scholarship workshop.com, a scholarship and college information site, and sponsor of the *Leading the Future II* and *Ragins Braswell National Scholarships*.

Contact Marianne Ragins using any of the following sources:

- www.scholarshipworkshop.com
- www.facebook.com/scholarshipworkshop
- www.twitter.com/ScholarshipWork
- www.shop.scholarshipworkshop.com

Index

2-2 program, 98
3-1 program, 98
3-2 program, 98
3-3 Law Program, 103

Academic advisement center, 26–28
  guidelines for using, 27–28
  reasons for consulting, 26
Academic advisors
  assistance in choosing major, 36
  as campus resource, 26
  preparation for meeting with, 37–39
  as source for funding opportunities, 187
Academic support services, 34
Advertising, for student entrepreneurs, 157
Advanced Internet search, 70, 139, 190, 194
Advisors. *See* academic advisors
AIESEC. *See* International Association of Students in Economics and Commerce (AIESEC)
AIFS. *See* American Institute for Study Abroad (AIFS)
Alcohol, 33-34, 124, 203
All I Really Need to Know about Life I Learned in Kindergarten (Fulghum), 225
Allen, Jany Kay
  on cooperative education, 71-72
Alpha Chi, 107
Alpha Lambda Delta, 107
Alumni association, 187,198
American Institute for Study Abroad (AIFS), 92
American University, 147

Annualcreditreport.com, 182
Annual fee, 176, 179-180
Annual percentage rate (APR), 178–179
Antioch University, 62
Applied learning, 62–83
  benefits of, 62–66
    contacts, 63
    decision tool, 65
    enhanced knowledge, 65
    friends, 66
    mentors, 64
    money, 63
    possible job offers, 65
    references, 63-64
    scholarship aid, 66
    technical skills, 64-65
    travel, 64
    work experience, 62-63
  cooperative education, 70-72
    consumer/business products opportunities, 81-82
    consumer/business services opportunities, 82-83
    finance opportunities, 77
    government opportunities, 75-76
    hospitality opportunities, 83
    media/arts/entertainment opportunities, 78-80
    non-profit opportunities, 74-75
    retail opportunities, 77
    student highlight, 71-72
    technology opportunities, 80-81
  directed individual study (DIS), 74
  experiential learning, 66
  internships, 66-70
    career center assistance with, 69

consumer/business products
opportunities, 81-82
consumer/business services
opportunities, 82-83
finance opportunities, 77
government opportunities, 75-
76
hospitality opportunities, 83
media/arts/entertainment
opportunities, 78-80
non-profit opportunities, 74-75
retail opportunities, 77
technology opportunities, 80-81
occupational learning, 66
reading courses, 74
research programs, 72-73
structure, 72
student highlight, 73-74
summer jobs/programs, 72
Apps, 44, 177, 199
APR. *See* annual percentage rate
(APR)
Association of College Honor
Societies, 110
Associations, as networking
opportunities, 140
Associations on the Net, 114, 140,
190
Au pair, 87
Avery, Charity
advice to high school students,
220
on extracurricular activities, 105

Bankrate.com, 168, 180, 181
Bates College, 31
Baylor University, 44
Beloit College, 97
Bennett, Jeannette, 220
Bernard D. Hendricks
Undergraduate Honors Conference,
102

Blevins, Spencer, 220
Blue-chip stock portfolio, 169-173
brokers, 171-172
choosing stocks, 170
company performance assessment,
169-170
direct stock purchases, 172-173
dollar cost averaging, 170
investment clubs, 173
registration, 172
reinvesting in, 172
researching companies, 170
terms, 170-171
blue-chip stocks, 171
dividend reinvestment plan
(DRIP), 170
optional cash purchase plan
(OCP), 170
Boston College, 102
Brokers, 171-172
Brown, Hodari Pilli Tourre
on internships, 67
what I wish I knew before college,
217-218
Buckholtz, David
on benefits of competitions, 99
on getting most from classes,
46-47
Bucknell University, 47
Business cards, 143-144
Buying Stocks Without a Broker
(Carlson), 171

Campus Compact, 131
Campus jobs, 130
benefits of, 129-130
student highlight, 132
work study, 130-131
Campus ministry, 114-115
Campus network center, 34
Campus resources, 18-31
academic advisement center, 26

guidelines for using, 27–28
reasons for consulting, 18
career/development center, 18–26
  acquainting yourself with, 24-26
  assistance in choosing major, 25
  goals of, 19
  importance of, 24
  internship assistance, 24,25
  registering, 19-23
for special issues, 33-36
  academic support services, 34
  campus network center, 34
  child development center, 34
  counseling and student development center, 33
  disability support services, 34
  drug education center, 33
  multicultural and resource center, 34
  self-development center, 34
  student leadership center, 35
  student support services, 34-35
  university ombudsman, 33
  women's studies and resource center, 34
health education center, 30
library, 28–29
  access to other university libraries, 29
new students center, 30
service learning center, 30-31
student health center, 30
student union, 29-30
top places to find upon arrival, 31-32
university information services, 30
writing center, 26
Career fairs, 139-140
Careerbuilder.com, 20
Career/development center, 18–26
  See also jobs
  acquainting yourself with, 24-26
  assistance in choosing major, 25
  goals of, 19
  importance of, 24
  internship assistance, 24,25
  registering, 19-23
Cargill, Jaime, 218
Carlson, Charles B., 171
Carter, Shawn, 45
Cash advance fee, 180
CDs. *See* certificates of deposit (CDs)
Center for new students, 30
Center for service learning, 30-31
Certificates of deposit (CDs), 164, 168
Chang, Ashley
  on activities beyond classroom, 41
  on fun experiences, 127
  what I wish I knew before college, 217
Charge cards, 174, 175, 181. *See also* credit cards
Child development center, 34
CIEE. *See* Council on International Educational Exchange (CIEE)
Classes, getting most from, 43-50
  student highlight, 46-47
  tips for, 45-46
  university highlight, 47
Cohen, Fraya, 201

College Consortium for International Studies, 92
College education
  cost of, 14
  facets of, 16
  opportunities available with, 15-16, 225
College preparation, 214-224
  campus advice from college students and recent grads, 219-221
  keys to, 221-224
  what I wish I knew before college, 214-219
College recruitment conferences, 138-139
Communication. *See also* interpersonal skills
  importance of effective, 151
  interviewing skills, 153-154
  leadership skills, 154-155
  oratorical skills, 152-153
  university highlight, 155
  writing skills, 153
Community service, 131-132. *See also* volunteering
  organizations, 131-132
  student highlight, 132
Company-issued credit card, 180
Competitions, 98-101
Conferences, 102
Contests, 98-102, 130, 133, 144, 162, 186, 209
Convenience card, 180-181
Cooperative education (Co-op), 62-63, 191-192, 212
  consumer/business products opportunities, 81-82
  consumer/business services opportunities, 82-83
  finance opportunities, 77
  government opportunities, 75-76
  hospitality opportunities, 83
  media/arts/entertainment opportunities, 78-80
  non-profit opportunities, 74-75
  retail opportunities, 77
  student highlight, 71-72
  technology opportunities, 80-81
Council on International Educational Exchange (CIEE), 84–86
  contact information, 92
  scholarships for study abroad, 91
Counseling and student development center, 33
Cover letters, 145
Credit cards, 174-183. *See also* charge cards; credit report
  as bad idea for funding education, 185
  as college pitfall, 204-205
  common mistakes, 175-178
  department store, 176
  role in establishing good credit, 174
  terms, 178-181
    annual fee, 179-180
    annual percentage rate (APR), 176, 178-179
    cash advance fee, 180
    company-issued credit card, 180
    convenience card, 180-181
    grace period, 179
    third party credit cards, 181
    travel and entertainment charge card, 180-181
    variable rate, 179
  tip for handling, 205
Credit report. *See also* credit cards
  importance of, 174
  monitoring, 182
  annualcreditreport.com, 182

Credit unions, 164-165
Crook, Amy, 177
Cuernavaca Language School, 94
Cuservicecenter.com, 165
CVS Caremark Corporation, 81

Degree audit, 27, 40, 54, 202
Directed individual study (DIS), 14, 74
Disability support services, 34
Dividend reinvestment plan (DRIP), 170
Dogsofthedow.com, 170
Dollar cost averaging, 170
Dominion Resources, 173
Donnelly, Mark, 36-37
Double major, 97-98
Drexel University, 62
DRIP. *See* dividend reinvestment plan (DRIP)
Drug education center, 33
Dual enrollment, 223

Early admission programs, 103
Earthwatch, 90
E. I. du Pont de Nemours & Co., 81
Encyclopedia of Associations, 140, 189
Entertainment, 124–128
  benefits of, 124
  campus events, 126-128
  defined, 124
  in dormitory, 127
  exercise, 127
  Greek organizations, 125-126
    advantages of membership, 126
    networking opportunities, 126
  parties, 117, 126, 127, 203
  special interest clubs, 125
  country of origin, 125
  cultural heritage, 125

regional, 125
sports, 126-127
student union, 127
Entrepreneurship, student, 156-162
  advertising, 157
  advice, 158
  mini beauty salon, 160
  product-based business, 158-159
  professional service, 161
  real estate, 160-161
  service business, 159
  storage service, 161
  typing service, 161
  student highlight, 161-162
  understanding start-up costs, 158-159
Events, on campus, 49, 107, 125-128, 209
Exchange programs
  international, 88, 93
  university, 96-97
Exercise, 127
Experiential learning, 66
Extracurricular activities, 105-116
  benefits of, 105-106
  campus ministry, 114-115
  finding, 107
  fraternities, 108-110
  honorary recognition societies, 108-110
  leadership skills development, 106, 107
  professional organizations, 112-114
  as scholarship consideration opportunity, 107
  scholastic honor societies, 108
  sororities, 108-110
  spiritual organizations, 114-115
  sports, 110-111
  student highlight, 112

Exxon Corporation, 171, 172

Facebook, 19, 52, 66, 74, 87, 107, 108, 112, 113, 116, 120, 121, 137, 139, 142, 160, 193, 199, 207, 208, 209, 210, 212, 217, 222
Faculty. *See* professors
Farming, 90
Fellowships, 55, 64, 65, 107, 142, 191, 194
Field research, 90
Finaid.org, 186
Financial aid
  additional funding, 186-196
    academic advisor, 187
    academic departments, 187
    alumni association, 187
    church/religious organization, 187
    civic organization, 187
    community organization, 187
    contests, 186
    employer, 194
    financial aid office, 130, 191
    interest-related financial aid, 191
    major-related financial aid, 187
    merit scholarships, 186
    minor-related financial aid, 193
    print resources/books, 186
    service scholarships, 187
    tuition reimbursement, 194
    work study, 187
  grants
    for service to organizations, 191
  scholarships

Greek organizations and, 194
  study abroad, 91
  professional organization membership and, 114
student loans, 183-185
  accumulating multiple, 205
  alternative loan repayment, 184-185
  credit cards versus, 185
  loan repayment, 183-184
  subsidized, 183
  unsubsidized, 183
  exploring other options, 183-185
Florida Agricultural and Mechanical University, 24, 73, 91, 102, 126, 129, 155, 161, 230
Follow-up letters, 143, 146, 149
Ford, Hayley
  on combating loneliness, 198
  on networking, 136
  on romantic relationships, 119
  on studying abroad, 92
  on time management, 51
Forums, 103-104
Fraternities, 108-110
  business, 108-109
  communication, 109
  economics, 108-109
  engineering, 109-110
  finance, 108-109
  humanities, 110
  language, 109
  math, 109
  medicine, 109
  music, 110
  nursing, 109
  pharmacy, 109
  science, 109
  social science, 110
Fulghum, Robert, 225
Fun, 124-128

benefits of, 124

campus events, 126-128

defined, 124

in dormitory, 127

exercise, 127

Greek organizations, 125-126

  advantages of membership, 126

  networking opportunities, 126

parties, 117, 126, 127, 203

special interest clubs, 125

  country of origin, 125

  cultural heritage, 125

  regional, 125

sports, 126-127

student union, 127

Georgia Institute of Technology, 62, 71

Getting Started in Mutual Funds (Hall), 167

Gilchrist, Tavia Evans

  on credit cards, 175-176

  on relationships as college pitfall, 204

  on studying abroad, 91-92

  what I wish I knew before college, 215-216

Giovanni, Nikki, 103

Google Hangouts, 224

Government opportunities, 75-76

GPA. *See* grade point average (GPA)

Grace period, 179

Grade point average (GPA), 15, 50, 51, 54-56

  boosting, 55-61

    good study habits and, 60-61

    strategies for, 57-59

    understanding calculation, 56

  importance of maintaining, 55

Grades

  credit card reward points and, 181

  getting good, 57-59

  maintaining, 55

  strategies for making best, 57–59

  time management and, 50, 53

Graduate and professional school days, 142

Graduation, path to, 40, 50,51, 53, 202

Grant, Angela, 73

Grants. *See also* financial aid.

  based on service to organizations, 191

Habitat for Humanity International, 40, 131

Hall, Alvin D., 167

He, Dianna

  on investments, 164

  on time management, 52

Health education center, 30

Hicks, Dave

  on romantic relationships, 119

  on volunteering abroad, 90

High school students, college preparation for, 214-223

  campus advice from college students and recent grads, 219-221

  keys to, 221-223

  what I wish I knew before college, 214-219

Hobbies, 222

Honorary recognition societies, 108–110

  business, 108-109

  communication, 109

  economics, 108-109

  engineering, 109-110

  finance, 108-109

  humanities, 110

language, 109
math, 109
medicine, 109
music, 110
nursing, 109
pharmacy, 109
science, 109
social science, 110
Honors programs, 101-102
Husbands, Erin Elizabeth
  advice to high school students,
    220-221
  on assistance with difficult
    classes, 57
  on partying as college pitfall,
    203-204
  on study rhythm, 60
  what I wish I knew before
    college, 214-215
Hyllengren, Janice, 218-219

IAPA. *See* International Au Pair
  Association (IAPA)
IFRE. *See* Institute for Field
  Research Expeditions (IFRE)
IIE. *See* Institute of International
  Education (IIE)
Immersion programs, 93-94
iNext, 85
Information sessions, 141-142
Informational interviews, 154
Institute for Field Research
  Expeditions (IFRE), 88-89
Institute of International Education
  (IIE), 93
Intensive language study, 93-94
Interdisciplinary programs, 102-103
International Association of Students
  in Economics and Commerce
  (AIESEC), 88
International Au Pair Association
  (IAPA), 87

International experience, 84-95
  au pair, 87
  basics, 84-86
    airfares, 86
    Eurail passes, 86
    planning, 85-86
    student identity card, 85-86
    travel insurance, 85
  immersion programs, 93-94
  intensive language study, 94-95
  international internships, 87-88
  overseas job opportunities, 87-
    88
  study abroad, 91-93
    benefits, 91
    considerations, 91
    financial aid for, 91
    sampling of programs, 92-
      93
    scholarships for, 91-92
    student highlight, 91-92
  volunteering abroad, 88-90
    farming, 90
    field research, 90
    student highlight, 90
    work camps, 89-90
International internships, 87-88
International Student Exchange
  Program (ISEP), 93
International Student Identity Card,
  85-86
International Student Travel
  Confederation (ISTC), 85
International Studies Abroad, 93
International Volunteer Programs
  Association (IVPA), 88
Internet
  access, 29, 31
  advanced Internet search, 70,
    139, 190, 194
  finding company internships
    on, 70

Internet Public Library, 114, 140
Internships, 62-83, 74-83,
  144, 147, 154, 209, 212-213, 222,
  benefits of, 62-66
  career center assistance with, 69
  consumer/business products
    opportunities, 81-82
  consumer/business services
    opportunities, 82-83
  finance opportunities, 77
  government opportunities, 75-
    76
  hospitality opportunities, 83
  media/arts/entertainment
    opportunities, 78-80
  non-profit opportunities, 74-75
  reasons to get an internship,
    212-213
  retail opportunities, 77
  student highlight, 71-72
  technology opportunities, 80-81
  types of, 67
Interpersonal skills, 151-155. *See
  also* communication
  importance of developing, 151
  interviewing skills, 153-154
  leadership skills, 154-155
  oratorical skills, 152-153
  university highlight, 155
  writing skills, 153
Interviewing skills, 153-154
Interviews
  informational, 154
  as networking opportunities,
    154
Introductory letters, 143, 145-146,
  148
Investment clubs, 173
Investment objectives, 166
Investments, 44, 163-168
  certificates of deposit (CDs),
    163, 164, 168

class, 44
  credit unions, 164-165
  mutual funds, 165-167
    classifications, 165-166
    described, 165
    terms related to, 166
  relationship with financial
    institution, 165
  savings bonds, 163, 164, 167
  as safe investment, 167
  series EE, 167
  stocks, 169-171
ISEP. *See* International Student
  Exchange Program (ISEP)
ISTC. *See* International Student
  Travel Confederation (ISTC)
IVPA. *See* International Volunteer
  Programs Association (IVPA)

Jackson, Rondre, 134-135
  on campus jobs, 134-135
  college survival and enhancement
    tips, 134
Janiczek, Janel, 184
Jarrett, Ronald, 48
Jessica Kupferman, 209-211
  on social media, 209-211
  on Facebook, 210
  on Twitter, 210
  on vagebooking, 210
Job fairs, 138-139
Jobs. *See also* career/development
  center
  campus, 130
    benefits of, 129-130
    community service, 131-132
    gaining professional trade
      experience, 132-133
    volunteering, 131-132
    work study, 130-131
Johnson Controls, 172-173
Judge, Julia Rose

advice to high school students,
219
on combating loneliness, 197
on Greek organizations, 126
what I wish I knew before college,
215

Law-related classes, 44
LBD curriculum. *See* learning-by-
doing (LBD) curriculum
Leadership, 18
campus jobs and, 130
campus ministry, 114
extracurricular activities and,
105, 106
honors programs and, 102
international internships and,
88
skills development, 154-155
student leadership center, 35
university highlight, 155
Learning-by-doing (LBD)
curriculum, 30-31
Letters
cover, 145
follow-up, 143, 146, 149
introductory, 143, 145
thank you, 150
Library, 28–29
access to other university libraries,
29
computer resources, 28-29
importance of, 28
information use, 28
LinkedIn, 19, 23, 63, 66, 69, 74,
108, 113, 137, 140, 143, 144,
151, 207, 212
Load, 166
Loneliness
as college pitfall, 204
combating, 15, 197-200

getting involved on campus,
198-199
strategies for, 197-200
tip to remember, 198-199
tip for dealing with, 204
Lopez, Roberto, Jr.
advice to high school students,
221
on extracurricular activities, 106-
107
what I wish I knew before
college, 216-217
Louise Harber/Foreign Language
Study Abroad Service, 94
Loyola University, 98
Lyons, Daniel
advice to high school students,
220
on alcohol as biggest college
pitfall, 203
on combating loneliness, 200
what I wish I knew before
college, 216

Major. *See* also minor
choosing, 36-42, 213
based on other's wishes, 201
career/development center and,
25
effect on career choice, 41
student highlight, 41
tips, 36-41
double, 97-98
Management 101, 47
Management fees, 166
Mehtar, Amelia
on extracurricular activities, 106
what I wish I knew before college,
216
Merit scholarships, 186
Michigan State University, 31
Miles, Deneige Kay, 218

Miller, John, 47
Minor, 65, 98. *See also* major
Mitchell, Ivy, 102
Monster.com, 20, 25
MonsterTRAK (web site), 69
Multicultural and resource center, 34
Mutual Fund Education Alliance, 167
Mutual funds, 165-167
  classifications, 165-166
    aggressive, 165, 166
    aggressive growth, 166
    balanced, 165
    conservative, 165, 166
  described, 165
  terms related to, 166
    investment objectives, 166
    load, 166
    management fees, 166
    net asset value (N.A.V.), 166
    prospectus, 167
    return, 166

NACE. *See* National Association of Colleges and Employers (NACE)
NAIC. *See* National Association of Investors Corporation (NAIC)
National Association of Colleges and Employers (NACE), 71
National Association of Investors Corporation (NAIC), 173
N.A.V. *See* net asset value (N.A.V.)
Neely, George, 49
Net asset value (N.A.V.), 166
Networking, 136-155. *See also* professional development
  associations, 140
  benefits of, 136
  career fairs, 139-140
  college recruitment conferences, 138-139

  defined, 136
  faculty and staff, 142
  graduate and professional school days, 142
  importance of interpersonal skills development, 151
  information sessions, 141-142
  informational interviews, 154
  interviews, 140-141
  job fairs, 138-139
  receptions, 137-138
  sources, 151
  through special interest clubs, 125
  tools, 143-146, 148-150
    address books, computerized, 146
    business cards, 143-144
    contact lists, computerized, 146
    cover letters, 145
    follow-up letters, 146, 149
    introductory letters, 145, 148
    résumés, 20-23, 144
    thank you letters, 150
New students, center for, 30
No-Load Stocks: How to Buy Your First Share & Every Share Directly From the Company (Carlson), 171

Occupational learning, 66
Occupational Outlook Handbook, 37, 39, 184
Optional cash purchase plan (OCP), 170
Oratorical skills, 152-153
Overseas job opportunities, 87-90

Parties, 117, 125, 126-127, 202-203
Pastimes, 126-128
Peterson's Guide to Scholarships, Grants, and Prizes, 186
Philip M. Dorr Alumni and Friends

Endowment Investment Fund, 44

Pitfalls, top ten, 201-206

choosing major based on other's wishes, 201

credit card mishandling, 204-205

getting off track with schedule, 202

letting relationships rule college life, 204

loneliness, 204

mismanagement of time, 202

multiple student loans, 205

partying too much, 202-203

putting off paying college costs, 205-206

trusting too easily, 202-203

waiting to ask for help, 201-202

Points of Light Foundation, 132

Price, Scott, 161-162

Procter & Gamble, 172

Professional development, 136-155. *See also* networking

importance of, 136

interviewing skills, 153-154

leadership skills, 154-155

oratorical skills, 152-153

university highlight, 155

writing skills, 153

Professional organizations, 112-114

benefits of membership, 113-114

departmental clubs, 113

scholarship opportunities, 114

Professional trade experience, 132-133

Professors, 47-49

advice, 49

consultations, 49

free professional services offered by, 48

as networking source, 142

as valuable information source, 48

Prospectus, 167

Reading courses, 74

Reading skills, 221

Receptions, 137-138

Relationships. *See* romantic relationships

Research programs, 72-73

structure, 72

student highlight, 73-74

Résumés, 20-23, 144

Return, 166

Robinson, AJ, on community service, 132

Romantic relationships, 119-123

Roommates, 116-118

Roth IRA, 164

Rusczyk, Richard, 119

Salaries, 37, 133, 140, 184

Salary.com, 37, 39, 184

Sallie Mae, 184, 185

Savings accounts, 163, 164, 168

Savings bonds, 163, 164, 167

Scarboro, Jordan

on getting most from professors, 49

on research programs, 73-74

what I wish I knew before college, 215

Schedule, staying on, 53-54

Scholarship Monthly Planner, The, 223

Scholarships, 66, 223. *See also* grants; student loans

for additional funding, 186-196

based on service to organizations, 187

extracurricular activities as opportunities for, 107

Greek organizations and, 194

merit, 186
professional organization
   membership and, 113
study abroad, 91
Scholastic honor societies, 108
School for International Training,
   93
Schorn, Stephen
   on good study habits, 61
   on roommates, 117
Self-development center, 34
Series EE savings bonds, 167
Service learning
   center for, 30-31
   colleges with successful programs,
   31
Sharebuilder.com, 171
Shareholder investment plans (SIPs),
   171
SIPs. *See* shareholder investment
   plans (SIPs)
Six P's, 28
Sororities, related to field of study,
   108-110
Social media, 156, 157, 199, 207-
   211
   as negative distraction, 207
   boon to personal life, 207
   cleaning up, 208
   Facebook, 19, 52, 66, 74, 87, 107,
      108, 112, 113, 116, 120, 121,
      137, 139, 142, 160, 193, 199,
      207, 208, 209, 210, 212, 217,
      222
   for fun, 209
   for help, 210
   for scholarships and financial
      aid, 208
   for jobs, 208-209
   Google Hangouts, 224
   Jessica Kupferman, 209-211
   LinkedIn, 19, 23, 63, 66, 69, 74,

108, 113, 137, 140, 143, 144,
   151, 207, 212
   on college romance, 120
   on getting to know people, 199
   on helping or hurting your
      college life, 207-211
   on vagebooking, 210
   Pinterest, 87
   Twitter, 19, 66, 74, 87, 108, 113,
      116, 121, 137, 193, 199, 207,
      208, 209, 210, 212, 222, 223
   Twitterview, 154
   YouTube, 19, 87, 208, 209, 222
Speaking skills. *See* oratorical skills
Special interest clubs, 125
   country of origin, 125
   cultural heritage, 125
   regional, 125
   sports, 126-127
Spelman College, 96-97
Spiritual organizations, 114-115
Spitler, Bing, 139, 145-146
Sports, 126-127
STA Travel, 86
St. Gallen Wings of Excellence
   Award, 99, 101
Staff, as networking source, 142
Stocks
   blue-chip stocks, 171
   brokers, 171-172
   choosing stocks, 170
   company performance assessment,
      169-170
   direct stock purchases, 172-173
   dollar cost averaging, 170
   investment clubs, 173
   registration, 172
   reinvesting in, 172
   researching companies, 170
   terms, 170-171
Strengths, identifying, 222
Student development center, 33

Student health center, 30
Student highlights
  campus jobs, 134-135
  choosing majors, 41
  classes, getting most from, 46-47
  community service, 132
  cooperative education, 71-72
  entrepreneurship, 161-162
  extracurricular activities, 112
  research programs, 73-74
  study abroad, 91-92
  volunteering, 90, 132
Student identity card, 85-86
Student leadership center, 35
Student loans, 183-185. *See also*
  grants; scholarships
  accumulating multiple, 205
  alternative loan repayment, 184-185
  credit cards versus, 185
  loan repayment, 183-184
  subsidized, 183
  unsubsidized, 183
  exploring other options, 183-185
Student support services, 34-35
Student union, 29-30, 127
Study abroad, 91-93
  benefits, 91
  considerations, 91
  financial aid for, 91
  sampling of programs, 92-93
  scholarships for, 91
  student highlight, 91-92
Study habits, developing good, 60-61
  determining what and how to study, 61
  learning study rhythm, 60-61
Study rhythm, 60-61

Subsidized loans, 183
Summer jobs/programs, 72
  consumer/business products opportunities, 81-82
  consumer/business services opportunities, 82-83
  finance opportunities, 77
  government opportunities, 75-76
  hospitality opportunities, 83
  media/arts/entertainment opportunities, 78-80
  non-profit opportunities, 74-75
  retail opportunities, 77
  student highlight, 71-72
  technology opportunities, 80-81

Test-taking skills, 223
Texas A & M University, 25, 90, 119
Thank you letters, 150
Third party credit cards, 181
Time management, 51-53
  as part of college preparation, 221
  advice from college student, 220
  importance of, 54
  steps, 52-53
  tip for, 202
  unwise, as college pitfall, 202
  what I wish I knew, 214
Top Performance (Ziglar), 105
Travel and entertainment charge card, 180-181
Travel discounts, for students, 86
Travel insurance, 85
Trujillo, Evelyn, 91
Tuition reimbursement, 194
Twitter, 19, 66, 74, 87, 108, 113, 116, 121, 137, 193, 199, 207, 208, 209, 210, 212, 222, 223
Twitterview, 154

University exchange programs, 96-97

University highlights
  classes, getting most from, 47
  interdisciplinary programs, 102-103
  networking, 156
  professional development, 148
  university exchange programs, 97
University information services, 30
University of Cincinnati, 62
University ombudsman, 33, 118
Unsubsidized loans, 184
Upromise.com, 186
Upshaw, Ryan, 203

Variable rate, 180
Vault Guide to Top Internships, 69
Volunteering, 15. *See also* community service
    abroad, 88
    farming, 90
  field research, 90
  student highlight, 90
  work camps, 89-90
  on campus, 132-133
  organizations, 132-133
  student highlight, 133
Volunteers of America, 133

Washington Research Library Consortium (WLRC), 29
Washington Semester Program, 148
Weaknesses, identifying, 223
Winning Scholarships for College, 185, 186, 187, 191, 223, 227, 230
Who's Who Among Students in American Universities and Colleges, 101
WLRC. *See* Washington Research Library Consortium (WLRC)

Women's studies and resource center, 34
WOOF (World-Wide Opportunities on Organic Farms), 89
Work camps, 89-90
Work study, 131-132, 134, 188
Working the room, 139
Writing
  centers, 26, 154
  skills, 154, 222

Yahoo! Finance, 170
Young, Whitney, 24

Zig Ziglar Corporation, 54
Ziglar, Zig, 54, 105